The Victorians

A Beginner's Guide

ONEWORLD BEGINNER'S GUIDES combine an original, inventive, and engaging approach with expert analysis on subjects ranging from art and history to religion and politics, and everything in-between. Innovative and affordable, books in the series are perfect for anyone curious about the way the world works and the big ideas of our time.

aesthetics
africa
american politics
anarchism
animal behaviour
anthropology
anti-capitalism
aquinas
archaeology
art
artificial intelligence
the baha'i faith
the beat generation
the bible
biodiversity
bioterror & biowarfare
the brain
british politics
the Buddha
cancer
censorship
christianity
civil liberties
classical music
climate change
cloning
the cold war
conservation
crimes against humanity
criminal psychology
critical thinking
the crusades
daoism
democracy
descartes
dewey
dyslexia
energy
engineering
the english civil wars
the enlightenment
epistemology
ethics
the european union
evolution
evolutionary psychology
existentialism
fair trade
feminism
forensic science
french literature
the french revolution
genetics
global terrorism
hinduism
history
the history of medicine
history of science
homer
humanism
huxley
international relations
iran
islamic philosophy
the islamic veil
journalism
judaism
lacan
life in the universe
literary theory
machiavelli
mafia & organized crime
magic
marx
medieval philosophy
the middle east
modern slavery
NATO
the new testament
nietzsche
nineteenth-century art
the northern ireland conflict
nutrition
oil
opera
the palestine–israeli conflict
particle physics
paul
philosophy
philosophy of mind
philosophy of religion
philosophy of science
planet earth
postmodernism
psychology
quantum physics
the qur'an
racism
rawls
reductionism
religion
renaissance art
the roman empire
the russian revolution
shakespeare
shi'i islam
the small arms trade
sufism
the torah
the united nations
the victorians
volcanoes
the world trade organization
world war II

The Victorians

A Beginner's Guide

David Gange

ONEWORLD

A Oneworld Paperback Original

Published in North America, Great Britain and Australia by
Oneworld Publications, 2016

A CIP record for this title is available from the British Library

ISBN 978-1-78074-828-3
eISBN 978-1-78074-829-0

Typeset by Silicon Chips
Printed and bound in Great Britain
by Clays Ltd, St Ives plc

Oneworld Publications
10 Bloomsbury Street
London WC1B 3SR
England

For my students,
especially those whose ideas have
contributed to this book:
Elisabeth Murray, Emily Howells,
Millie Santry, Philippa Lane,
Patrick McGhee, Hannah Clarke, Hannah Witton,
Ruth Lindley, and Ellie Dobson.

Contents

1 Introducing the Victorians

The Condition of England, on which many pamphlets are now in the course of publication, and many thoughts unpublished are going on in every reflective head, is justly regarded as one of the most ominous, and withal one of the strangest, ever seen in this world.

Thomas Carlyle, *Past & Present* (1843)

New Queen, new age?

On 28 June 1838, almost exactly a year after the death of her uncle, King William IV, Queen Victoria was crowned in Westminster Abbey. William IV's coronation in 1831 had been the first to feature a procession by carriage through the streets of London. Victoria followed suit but took a far longer, almost circular, route. Londoners, as well as nearly half a million visitors to the capital, observed the royal parade in all its glory. Nobles and dignitaries from around the world were present to demonstrate their respect for the new Queen. Yet press reports often chose to focus not on aristocratic wealth or royal grandeur but on 'the dark and heaving masses' who lined the route. These crowds were 'full of eager expectation' but also carried a hint of threat in this politically unsettled era. Would the eighteen-year-old Queen be overwhelmed by the sight of these thronging masses? The Duchess of Sutherland was on hand to help her 'conceal … her emotions' and the procession's first port of call, the Ordnance Office, was manned by Royal Artillery in case 'the vast masses that pressed on all sides, deepening and accumulating', should give in to the unruly instincts of the mob.

This parade was the high point of an otherwise inauspicious coronation. The ceremony itself was unrehearsed, disorganized, and mishandled (the modern, micromanaged event, seen at the coronation of Elizabeth II, was, despite its medieval trappings, invented only in 1902). The young Queen spent much of the five-hour service, during which she wore three dresses, eating sandwiches from the altar of a side chapel. The traditional coronation banquet was not even held, and the mood was dampened by news of anti-royal protests held in Northern English cities such as Manchester and Newcastle. This was a ceremony too ostentatious for radicals, who required that the will of the people, not the monarch, be placed at the centre of public life, but too unspectacular for Tories, who demanded pomp to demonstrate royal authority.

This was also among the most unlikely coronations in British history. The young Victoria had been fifth in line just a few years earlier, but would have slipped further from the throne if any of her father's three brothers had fathered children who survived beyond infancy. Only a series of accidents – a strange destiny – had led to the events of 28 June. Many of Victoria's subjects believed strongly in the power of destiny (or 'providence' as Victorian religion styled it) to define personal and national fortunes, and by the time the Queen's fate had taken its course she was not just monarch of the United Kingdom of Great Britain and Ireland, Defender of the Faith, Princess of Hanover, and Duchess of Brunswick but also Queen of vast colonies and Empress of India. Britannia ruled an extraordinary number of waves.

As with most supposed destinies, there were substantial cracks in the impressive facade. Victoria's reign was as troubled as her coronation. Her accession took place at a time when the nation she ruled was divided. The gulf in wealth and resources between rich and poor was large and constantly increasing, while conflict between European powers remained probable despite the fragile settlements that followed the Napoleonic Wars. Disagreement raged over the nature of state and society: in most circles, 'democracy' remained a dirty word, while in some it was emerging as the rallying cry for a reformed politics, free from the elite domination and corruption of the old regime.

The young Queen, less conservative than her Tory uncle William IV, gave such hope to the champions of democracy that radical ballads were sung in her honour. In a parliamentary system where Whigs often favoured values that might loosely be termed liberal and Tories stood for conservative ideals, Victoria was a Whig monarch, with a Whig government. However, in 1838, it was not clear what direction the following decades would take. Would the 'deepening and accumulating' masses rise, as they had in France fifty years before, to demand a more substantial redrawing of politics than had been provided by the meek and mild Reform Act of 1832? Or would the powerful Tory contingent in Parliament embark on its golden age, strengthened by the controlled reform of the early 1830s, with its claim to represent Britain (symbolically rather than democratically) more credible than ever before?

The spell cast by the word 'Victorian'

This Queen's name gives us a term that conjures many vivid images: lace and crinoline, top hats and petticoats, steam trains and horse-drawn cabs. It suggests child labour in factories and mines, corporal and capital punishment, street crime, acceptance (even approval) of domestic abuse, and a stern religion that damned all but a few to hell. It suggests the mundane violence of the strap-wielding father and the infamous cruelty of Jack the Ripper. But maybe 'vivid' is the wrong word for these images since they reach us in shades of sepia and grey that befit the nostalgic and repressed Victorians of our imagination. This is the first era for which we possess a photographic record, and the peculiarities of the Victorians' efforts to negotiate their strange new technology informs our view of them. Morbidly, they photographed their dead. Earnestly, they did not dare to smile when photographed. Rigidly, they only very rarely betray small informalities in front of the lens. Lengthy exposure times necessitated the stiff formality that we too readily assume the Victorians to have embodied in everyday life.

In photographs, we see everything of these people except the colours; everything except the unguarded expressions that convey character; everything but what went on in their heads. These photographs impress a caricature on our memories: an era that is close to us in time, yet in ethos and atmosphere is everything we are not. The Edwardians invented this image of the Victorians as their opposites, the 'other' against which they defined themselves. We have allowed this habit to persist. Where *we* nurture children, the Victorians exploited them; where *we* pursue equality in class and gender, the Victorians protected institutions that sustained inequality; where *we* are spontaneous, liberated, and funny, the Victorians were earnest, uptight, and humourless.

Many Victorians were, however, far more radical and progressive than those self-conscious Edwardians who made their name mud. Even in photographs, their formality could occasionally disappear, leaving strikingly modern individuals, as images recently discovered in the Northumberland Archives have demonstrated. In other words, it was because some Victorians defended institutions that oppressed the poor, women, or children that other Victorians assaulted these institutions with an aggression and enthusiasm that had never been seen before. Far from revelling in child exploitation, many Victorians demonstrated unprecedented commitment to the rights of children to education and protection from hard labour. The chief reason that a patriarchal, repressive, and literalist religion was defended with great vigour was that its worldview was now rivalled and threatened by liberal theologians, geologists, physicists, and, later, evolutionary biologists.

If we are to understand this strange period, we must do so through these contrasts and oppositions. We must recognize that the Victorians were not defined by what they agreed on, but by what they argued over. This was a society in which public debate took place on an unprecedented scale, drawing in far more of the population than ever before. The periodical press, in which much of this debate took place, was vast and flourished on a scale that we (with our relatively short list of major magazines, newspapers, and journals) find difficult to imagine. Across the century, the number of separate periodical titles cannot be counted in the hundreds, or even the thousands, but exceeded 130,000. In the millions of pages therein, countless questions were discussed countless times. Above all, this was a society that *argued*. It debated its every innovation. It interrogated the moral purpose of the sciences and the scientific basis of morals. It even argued about whether or not this was the most argumentative time and place in history. In disputes such as these, we will find 'the Victorians', a subtle and contradictory population, far more thoughtful, three-dimensional, and subversive than our stereotypes allow.

The Victorian self-image

One topic of intense argument in Victorian Britain was the term 'Victorian' itself. By the middle of Victoria's long reign, this adjective cast its spell over Victorians as much as it does over the twenty-first century. During the first twenty years of the period, the term 'Victorian' had not been in common use. Its rare appearances came largely in satire: it was used to mock those arrogant enough to assume that their own eccentricities could characterize an 'era'. From 1857 onwards, however, the term proliferated, its usage triggered by the twentieth anniversary of Victoria's accession. By the 1880s, it was subject to intense dispute throughout society.

From 1857 onwards, most who commented agreed that to speak of a Victorian age made sense. They insisted that the 1830s had not just seen the accession of a monarch, but also marked a distinctive break in British history: 'old things passed away, and behold, all things became new'. The 1857 article on 'Victorian Literature' from which this quote comes listed a host of things that made the 1830s into a 'new age' including the establishment of a railway network, the first instance of communication by telegraph (1837), the first steam-powered crossing of the Atlantic (1838), the first education grants, the introduction of a penny post, and the first matches (an important invention in cities lit by candle and gaslight). The author then listed the deaths, in quick succession between 1832 and 1836, of the major literary and philosophical figures of the preceding 'age': Goethe, Walter Scott, Samuel Taylor Coleridge, Charles Lamb, Hannah More, Jeremy Bentham, Thomas Malthus, James Mill, and Samuel Wilberforce (among many other celebrated names). With the Napoleonic Wars (1798–1815) a memory, and the 'bawdy' eighteenth century fading from view, writers such as the 'Victorian sage' Thomas Carlyle felt they had a chance to make a fresh start. For Carlyle, writing in 1837, there had been nothing noble in the frivolous eighteenth century at all until the 'grand universal suicide' accomplished in the French Revolution, which seemed to open up a new world – with new hopes and fears – before him and his serious-minded, Victorian, contemporaries.

VICTORIAN SAGES

This term describes a self-styled 'cultural aristocracy' who acted as guardians of Victorian high culture. They include:

- **Thomas Carlyle (1795–1881)**, author of *On Heroes and Hero Worship* (1841)
- **Matthew Arnold (1822–88)**, Chief Inspector of Schools, author of *Culture and Anarchy* (1869)
- **John Ruskin (1819–1900)** author of *Modern Painters* (1843–60)

These sages wrote stylish books and essays that took society to task for lacking high ideals. Some of their more concise works still make great reading, but their elitism can cause discomfort. In current usage, 'sage' is a deliberately pompous term that draws attention to the self-importance of this all-male cast. Other thinkers – e.g. George Eliot (Marian Evans) and Harriet Martineau – were their equals as writers but lacked the sages' social cachet.

This perception of a clean break persisted throughout Victoria's reign. For instance, an 1888 essay in *The Gentleman's Magazine* insisted that the 1830s were

> A time of singular activity and innovation in all departments of life. The prolonged reaction produced by the wild excesses of the first French Revolution was at last exhausting itself. Ideas of political advance that had been put aside for more than a generation began once more to be ardently and irrepressibly entertained. Democracy began to feel its strength and to make its strength felt … 'The world's great age' seemed beginning anew; 'the golden years' seemed returning. And in all directions, along with this political energy, both just before and just after 1832, there were accomplished new developments and signal discoveries.

This passage might appear triumphalist, yet it embodies the idea of contradiction and disagreement crucial to this argumentative moment. It even contains its own counter-argument by voicing, subtly, a key characteristic of the age: intense uncertainty. One repeated word is far more significant than it may at first appear: the great age 'seemed' to be beginning; the golden years 'seemed' to be returning. The article goes on to explore the ways in which appearances mislead; anyone reading about the Victorians will need to get used to this deceptiveness of surface appearances.

The question of whether improvements were real or illusory worried many Victorians. Increasing numbers of people from the 1830s onwards were painfully aware of the price paid for every incremental advance. This was an era of sensational social commentaries describing in vivid detail the horrific conditions that uncontrolled urban growth had generated; it was the era of novels, such as those of Dickens, which aimed to elucidate the experiences and meanings that lay behind the brute facts of social change, bringing the emotional consequences of poverty and hardship to general attention. This genre was soon given labels such as 'social problem' and 'condition of England' novel. In fact, this age might just as well be labelled 'Dickensian' as 'Victorian' given the influence of Dickens's characters and themes over subsequent images of the time. In the rise of this socially astute literature and the foundation of large public bodies devoted to assessing the evils attendant on progress, the self-scrutiny characteristic of the age was thought through and institutionalized. 'Victorian values' of philanthropy, education, and enfranchisement were being formulated but so too were Victorian characteristics of domination, control, and patriarchal discipline.

For God and empire

With an apparent self-assurance that verged on the megalomaniac, the Victorians sought to export their values around the world.

Through missionary movements, military escapades, and the Royal Navy, they aimed to take 'civilization' to the farthest-flung corners of the earth. With little understanding of the civilization that already existed in places where they exerted their military might, the British aimed to create recipients for their industrial production as well as their ideas. And so began the new dawn of the British Empire.

Through this idealistic aggression, the British Isles, once an insignificant North East Atlantic archipelago, gained a fleeting global significance. The height of this influence coincided with the late Victorian period. This means that what we make of the empire, with its blend of high ideals and ferocious brutality, is defined in part by what we make of the Victorians whose ideals and actions upheld it. This is one reason why the Victorians sustain so much interest, why big moral questions remain at the heart of any assessment of their identity, and why disagreements about who the Victorians were rest on our own politics as well as on matters of historical fact.

TIMELINE OF THE BRITISH EMPIRE

1600: Queen Elizabeth I grants a Royal Charter to the Governor and Company of Merchants of London Trading in the Indies (East India Company).

1620: *The Mayflower*, carrying the Pilgrim Fathers, arrives in the Americas.

1644: The East India Company constructs Fort St George in Madras.

1757–64: Seven Years' War. The East India Company takes control of Bengal, ejecting French interests in India.

1770: Captain Cook reaches Australia. Convicts soon begin to be shipped to Botany Bay.

1776: Expansion is matched by contraction: loss of American colonies in War of Independence.

1820: 5,000 British settlers arrive in Cape Town.

1831: Extinction of Tasmanian Aborigines after relocation by British troops.

1833: Argentinians are removed from Malvina Islands and British farmers settle there.
1839–42: First Anglo–Afghan War: the East India Company invade Afghanistan (also known as Auckland's Folly).
1845: First Anglo–Sikh War: conflict between the East India Company and the rulers of Punjab.
1854–6: War in the Crimea sees imperial powers face each other down in Eastern Europe.
1857: Indian Uprising. Also known as India's First War of Independence.
1858: India placed under direct control of the British government rather than the East India Company.
1867: Four former colonies unite to form the new nation of Canada, the first imperial 'Dominion'.
1879: Zulu War. Powerful resistance meets British attempts to unify Southern Africa.
1882: British occupation of Egypt: a supposedly anti-imperial Liberal government attempts to protect British interests in India by securing the Suez Canal.
1880s and 90s: 'Scramble for Africa' brings the majority of Africa into European empires.
1884: General Gordon, military leader and Protestant culture hero, killed at Khartoum.
1899: Outbreak of the Boer War. Strong Boer resistance to British military power represents the biggest shock to British confidence since 1857.

The empire was built on values that were specifically Christian. Imperial self-confidence saw millions of Protestant religious tracts circulated through India and Africa. In contrast, the fate of Victorian religion in Britain is often viewed as a story of loss and fragmentation. The period is caricatured with phrases like 'the age of doubt' or 'the crisis of faith'. This picture is best captured by the statistics of the 1851 census, which sent shockwaves through Britain with its revelation that only around a quarter of the population of England attended a Church of England service on the census Sunday. The contrast between an empire held together by

Christianity and a Christianity that was apparently falling apart at home is one of the great contradictions of this period.

In this small word, 'Victorian', an array of contrasts is captured. Intense religious enthusiasm seems to coexist with rampant secularization; growing middle-class wealth with poverty of the most extreme kind; a liberal vision of enfranchisement with Tory commitment to the established order; a Queen wielding immense power with millions of women confined to domestic duty; global vision with parochial insularity; a deeply traditional people who were Britain's most aggressive modernizers before the 1960s. As we embark on this book, we must not expect the Victorians to be simple or easily captured in generalizations: they left too much prose, poetry, art, and music for that to be plausible.

In 1918, Lytton Strachey made the best known of all statements on Victorian history: 'the history of the Victorian Age will never be written, we know too much about it'. Strachey was right. It is always worth remembering, however, that each of us knows a different Victorian age. The Victorians Margaret Thatcher attempted to resurrect in the early 1980s, captured by phrases like 'colossal advance', 'self-reliance', and 'general prosperity', were not the Victorians mocked by the satirical novelist Gail Carriger for their 'absurd … manners and ridiculous fashions … dictated by Vampires'. Nor were they the Victorians dismissed for their extreme sentimentality by Oscar Wilde – 'one must have a heart of stone to read the death of [Dickens's] little Nell without laughing' – or those free-thinking people praised as trailblazers when the Victorian naturalist Charles Darwin is conscripted by modern advocates of an exclusively scientific worldview.

This book aims to provide readers with a map of these many Victorians, steering a course between (or around) the caricatures of 'Victorian' as a byword for sentimentality or repression and of the Victorians as a people obsessed with progress at all costs, callously undermining the very foundations of society and plunging their poor into ever deeper poverty. The Victorians were all of these things and none, just as every stereotype of twenty-first-century societies reveals partial truths but does not even aspire to tell the whole truth. The nation and empire Victoria inherited from William IV was very different from the one that she left for Edward VII in 1901. It was not so much that the Victorians had transformed Britain, but that they were carried along on powerful tides of world history. These were tides they, for a little while, had seemed able to command. Extraordinary productivity seemed, briefly, to raise them above the accepted laws of economic development, but the world order of which they were part was crumbling long before the First World War proved its fragility.

'The great Victorian age is at an end'

Victoria's funeral echoed her coronation, yet it took place in a different social world. On a bitterly cold day in February 1901, her parade passed through the streets of London, witnessed by hundreds of thousands of people, only a handful of whom recalled her coronation. These were no longer the 'dark masses' of the 1830s – they were not 'the mob' but 'the public', though there were still vast social inequalities. Most notably, despite successful campaigns for male suffrage, more than half the adult population were still without a vote. On a smaller scale, the new Trade Unions were just beginning to find their feet. But all social classes were now assumed to be part of, rather than arrayed against, the political establishment: the newspapers voiced nothing comparable to their 1830s nervousness when describing the interaction of large crowds with royal dignitaries. Indeed, Victoria's death was met with an outpouring of national grief that was close to universal: this emotional farewell was depicted by the novelist John Galsworthy as 'supremely symbolical' and a 'tribute of an age to its own death'. The vast majority of working-class people read the conservative press rather than manning the new Trade Unions. Marxism, rife throughout Europe, was still surprisingly rare in Britain. As the historian Martin Hewitt has noted, even radicals 'participated without any great unease in the ceremonial of the loyal subject'. The Tory Prime Minister Benjamin Disraeli insisted in the 1880s that commitment to the values of imperial culture could unify the social classes in Britain; in 1901, he could still be argued to be right.

However, this was not an occasion without its own air of foreboding. In the funeral cortege, the new king, Edward VII, walked elbow to elbow with the German Kaiser despite the diplomatic tensions that were already brewing. When the funeral procession was ready to set off, the horses tethered to Victoria's coffin refused to pull it, behaving skittishly and dangerously because of a damaged harness. The monarchs of Britain and Germany shuffled uneasily in the cold, waiting for sailors from the Royal Navy to recover Britain's pride and take up the burden where horses had failed.

If Victoria's coronation had epitomized the uncertain condition of Britain in 1838, the troubles of her funeral parallelled in miniature the vexed state of Europe at the turn of the twentieth century. The continent's diplomatic structure had stressed and fractured, sabotaged by the nationalism that nineteenth-century cultures had encouraged. At the same time, the place of Europe within the world was becoming increasingly unclear. British self-confidence was crippled by the string of military failures that made up the second Boer War between 1899 and 1900; the response to this was a wave of patriotic fervour – christened in this period as 'jingoism' – of the crudest kind. It is perhaps because of the horrors that began to amass soon after Victoria's death, accumulating over the next half-century, that modern culture often chooses to remember the Victorians as naive, simple, and blinkered: reminiscent of children who are afraid of growing up. The task of this book is to ask what other Victorians we might choose to recall.

2

Sounds and sights of the city: experiencing the Victorian metropolis

> *Fog everywhere. Fog up the river, where it flows among green aits and meadows; fog down the river, where it rolls defiled among the tiers of shipping and the waterside pollutions of a great (and dirty) city … Fog creeping into the cabooses of collier-brigs; fog lying out on the yards, and hovering in the rigging of great ships; fog drooping on the gunwales of barges and small boats. Fog in the eyes and throats of ancient Greenwich pensioners, wheezing by the firesides of their wards; fog in the stem and bowl of the afternoon pipe of the wrathful skipper, down in his close cabin; fog cruelly pinching the toes and fingers of his shivering little 'prentice boy on deck. Chance people on the bridges peeping over the parapets into a nether sky of fog, with fog all round them, as if they were up in a balloon, and hanging in the misty clouds. Gas looming through the fog in divers places in the streets … The raw afternoon is rawest, and the dense fog is densest, and the muddy streets are muddiest near that leaden-headed old obstruction, appropriate ornament for the threshold of a leaden-headed old corporation, Temple Bar. And hard by Temple Bar, in Lincoln's Inn Hall, at the very heart of the fog, sits the Lord High Chancellor in his High Court of Chancery.*
>
> Charles Dickens, *Bleak House* (1853)

One of the features of Victorian Britain that draws most attention today is its appearance. Whether in dramatizations of Dickens, in films like *The Young Victoria*, or in subcultures such as steampunk, recreations or reimaginings of Victorian imagery are often carried out with awe-inspiring attention to detail. Whether set in the orderly stately home or disordered urban sprawl, they aim to capture the essence of the period (although this essence has changed from decade to decade, whether the 'dirty Victorians' favoured in 1940s films or the 'clean' equivalent of the 1980s). Raphael Samuel, in 'Who Calls So Loud? Dickens on Stage & Screen' in *Theatres of Memory: Past & Present in Contemporary Culture*, evokes these changing visions, from grotesque realism in constructions of a problematic and repulsive society in the mid-twentieth century, to a late twentieth-century version, which seeks to 'preserve' Victorian values and give viewers pleasure in lavish settings. All this evocation is fitting, since the teeming, fog-bound streets of Victorian cities were recognized at the time as a dizzying sensory extravaganza. Urban fogs could either be the stinking veil that hid the horrors of violent ulcers at the core of Britain, or the 'friendly fogs' that made cities atmospheric, enriching the promise of adventure.

NOVELISTS AND VICTORIAN LONDON

- Many of Charles Dickens's novels offer vivid depictions of London, from *Oliver Twist* (1838) to *David Copperfield* (1850) and *Our Mutual Friend* (1865).
- William Thackeray, *Vanity Fair* (1847–8), Anthony Trollope, *The Way We Live Now* (1875), Henry James, *A London Life* (1888), and George Gissing, *New Grub Street* (1891) all depict London society in perceptive and insightful ways.
- Arthur Conan Doyle's Sherlock Holmes stories (1887–1927) contain particularly vivid depictions of fog-wreathed streets and the city.
- Charles Kingsley's Chartist novel *Alton Locke* (1850) portrays poverty and radicalism in the city. Margaret Harkness's socialist novel *In Darkest London* (1889) provides a still fuller vision of destitution.

- Many other novels such as Wilkie Collins's *The Woman in White* (1859) take place between rural locations and London.
- However, some major novelists who lived in London preferred to provide urban readers with portraits of rural settings. The characters in George Eliot's 'scenes from provincial life', *Middlemarch* (1874), move to London only at the novel's close. Thomas Hardy's novels such as *The Return of the Native* (1878) depict rural southern England, styled by Hardy as 'Wessex'.
- Other novelists and poets went further and depicted alternative Londons. H.G. Wells's *The Time Machine* showed future London as a 'waste garden' ruined by time and human error, while William Morris's *The Earthly Paradise* asked its readers to envisage London 'small and white and clean', the Thames bordered not by factories but 'by its gardens green'. Richard Jefferies's *After London, or, Wild England* (1885) made a similar, though more disconcerting appeal: part I, 'The Relapse into Barbarism', begins, 'It became green everywhere in the first spring, after London ended, so that all the country looked alike'.

Glasgow, Manchester, Liverpool, and London were the most extreme of these burgeoning conurbations. London, by the 1830s, was the most written-about city in the world, yielding millions of words each year concerning its smells, sights, and sounds, and the emotions it conjured. The Victorian city's intense impact on the senses ranged from the competitive clamour of innumerable street performers to the ever-more elaborate window displays of the lavish new department stores and the visceral impact of the world-famous stench of 'Father Thames' ('that stream of moving sewage'). For better or worse, London was experienced in the most immediate ways and recorded in phenomenal detail.

Music halls or public executions, where the full range of social classes were brought into contact, produced masses of observational literature. Some of this painted London as the largest and most degraded 'heathen city in modern Europe'; some held it up as a glittering example of the benefits of progress. The well-to-do deplored the smells and coarse manners of the poor, while working people ridiculed the elaborate fashions of the leisured classes, whose hair could be sculpted into massive forms so prohibitively cumbersome that its sole function was to demonstrate its wearer's freedom from practical considerations of work.

Not just journalists or social commentators but also novelists created vivid images of London's streets. From Charles Dickens to George Gissing, these were often lurid and disturbing. The urban fog harboured ragged pocket pickers like Oliver Twist, burly house-breakers like Bill Sykes, and damaged "fallen women" like Nancy. Other novelists such as Anthony Trollope preferred to document high society, creating vivid anatomies of the arcane hierarchies of the better-off. Some of the greatest novelists – George Eliot in *Daniel Deronda* (1876) or William Thackeray in *Vanity Fair* (1848) – drew psychological and narrative interest from the juxtaposition of London's extremes. The well-to-do Daniel Deronda finds himself drawn into the travails of London's disempowered after saving an impoverished young Jewish woman from drowning. Thackeray's destitute orphan, Becky Sharp, works her way into the alien world of turtle-eating and champagne-swilling aristocrats. The pathos or humour that emerges from collisions between silver-spoon luxury and the striving, aspiring, but disempowered poor is the emotional engine room of portrait after portrait of life in Victorian London. This chapter will therefore fuse the London of the novelist with the work of social commentators – such as Edwin Chadwick, William Booth, and Friedrich Engels – who combined statistics, maps, and descriptive prose to alert their comfortable publics to the plight of the urban dispossessed.

These two sets of sources make a happy combination, since this was an era of searching social exploration in non-fiction, as well as the heyday of sympathetic realism in the novel. Both aimed to interpret the inner meanings behind the surface appearances of new urban spaces. Authors endeavoured to intervene in a city in crisis by promoting better understanding of its inhabitants.

They borrowed each other's techniques and ideas in order to hammer home the sensory catastrophe of the slums: the overpowering stench of flowing effluvia, the horror show of human bodies twisted by overwork, and the constant hellish noise of industry.

Street sights, sounds, and smells

Victorian London was a mess. This chaos was not just an aesthetic issue: it also promoted the spread of disease. Firstly, there was tuberculosis: the biggest killer. This ailment had been rare in rural communities, but now seemed so inevitable and unstoppable that it received little analysis from medical experts or social reformers. Then there was typhus, known as 'the poor man's disease', which was quickly associated with squalor and bad sanitation and was the cause of several major epidemics in the first half of the century. More frightening still was the new horror of cholera. The sickness was carried from Bengal at the beginning of the 1830s, William Sproat of Sunderland gaining an unlikely celebrity as its first victim in Britain. Cholera epidemics killed on a massive scale (53,000 died in 1848–9 alone). Of all diseases, this generated the greatest panic because outbreaks were not confined to squalid, overcrowded areas: carried in water, cholera threatened the middle classes too. By the early Victorian period, Londoners were exposed to disease and sickness on a scale not seen since the Black Death half a millennium earlier. The city's smells and overcrowding therefore developed more direct association with death and disease than ever before. Victorians became more sensitive to the smells of their cities than any of their predecessors.

In 1837, London shared its chaotic and frightening qualities with other expanding industrial capitals: none had found answers to the problems of urban filth, none had made sense of the spread of disease, and none had imposed order on streets that were transformed by massive population growth. However, by the 1880s, London's ramshackle thoroughfares made an unsavoury contrast with the dazzling new boulevards of central Paris. Berlin and Vienna, too, had taken steps to impose order on sprawling cityscapes, but London, despite the building of the world's first sewers, remained a mess. Money had been spent not on the wholesale reorganization of urban space, but on the building of docks and on the railway boom. More ships than ever carried extravagantly valuable loads down urban rivers that were still afloat with stinking waste.

By the end of the century, a different kind of literature recorded this urban chaos. Voyeuristic visitors from abroad increasingly flocked to the metropolis, often revelling in the smuttier side of the fastest-growing city in the world. Parisian flaneurs, most famously Charles Baudelaire, had made the sleazy side of cities an aesthetic subject in the mid-century, but the late Victorian years were the heyday of this thrill-seeking, pleasure-drunk gaze. The sketch of London in this section therefore takes us from the horror of 1830s Londoners at the squalor and poverty in their midst, to the more detached perspective of international visitors to the metropolis which made a celebrity of the faceless Jack the Ripper.

One of the earliest and most significant examples of modern imaginative urban reportage coincides with the beginning of the Victorian period. This was Charles Dickens's series of 'street sketches' published pseudonymously as *Sketches by Boz, Illustrative of Every-day Life and Every-day People* (1836). These vignettes already record isolation amidst crowds and the dislocating, disconnected feel of the urban landscape: 'Tis strange', writes Boz in 'Thoughts about People', 'with how little notice, good, bad or indifferent, a man may live or die in London. He awakens no sympathy in the breast of any single person; his existence is a matter of interest to no one save himself'.

Boz is a 'speculative pedestrian' with 'an extraordinary partiality for lounging about the streets'. His sketches often make the city itself their focus. They depict 'the cold solitary desolation' of silent streets at dawn, or the main thoroughfares at noon 'thronged with a vast concourse of people, gay and shabby, rich and poor, industrious and idle', or the evening city 'when the heavy lazy mist, which hangs over every object, makes the gas-lamps look brighter and the brilliantly lighted shops more splendid'.

Boz embarks on long solitary walks, but also, with enthusiasm, takes to the new omnibus, which offers an 'extensive field for amusement and observation'. This is a city experienced visually, and perceptions of its superficial characteristics are recorded in loving detail. As Dickens noted on numerous occasions, without London as the frame in which he observed the bustle of life, he was bereft of the stimulations that inspired the vivid character portraits in his novels.

Boz was one of several fictional observers who embodied a specifically male gaze calculated to reveal the city's soul. As the literary scholar Deborah Nord wrote, this masculine spectator

> Passes invisibly through the crowd and then behind the facades of buildings, extending … a 'potent and benignant hand, which takes off the housetops and shows the shapes and phantoms' within. He discerns the patterns of social relations that remain hidden to the uninitiated or the indifferent; he is investigator and theorist of poverty, disease, and class difference.

These visions of the city were not unique in their efforts to arouse middle-class sentiments. Among the earliest and most influential attempts to increase awareness were the essays of the enterprising playwright and journalist Henry Mayhew. A correspondent for a newspaper, the *Morning Chronicle*, Mayhew plunged repeatedly into a world that few middle-class Victorians knew anything about: the East End slums that housed the labouring poor. He interviewed hundreds of individuals whose ways of life proved deeply shocking to his readers. These included prostitutes, but also 'pure finders' who collected dog faeces to sell to tanners, and 'mudlarks' who spent their lives scouring the foul fringes of the Thames for fragments of coal, wood, and rope to sell as scrap. Mayhew's prose was novelistic in its drama, detail, and emotional characterization. When he described a marketplace, for instance, it was no less sensory than a Dickensian scene setting:

> The pavement and the road are crowded with purchasers and street-sellers ... Little boys, holding three or four onions in their hand, creep between the people, wriggling their way through every interstice, and asking for custom in whining tones, as if seeking charity. Then the tumult of the thousand different cries of the eager dealers, all shouting at the top of their voices, at one and the same time, is almost bewildering ... 'Buy, buy, buy, buy, buy – bu-u-uy!' cries the butcher ... 'Come and look at 'em! Here's toasters!' bellows one with a Yarmouth bloater stuck on a toasting-fork. 'Penny a lot, fine russets,' calls the apple woman: and so the Babel goes on.

Mayhew's articles for the *Morning Chronicle* were collected into one of the leading texts of social exploration – *London Labour and the London Poor* (1851) – and its most visceral passages became among the most quoted texts of the century, reprinted in radical newspapers and adapted by novelists, playwrights, and Christian Socialist poets. The notoriety, and impact, of the book was increased by Mayhew's embrace of new technology: engravings from daguerreotypes (one of the first forms of photography) gave his readers immediate visual accompaniments to his vivid prose. In reviewing *London Labour and the London Poor*, William Thackeray accounted for its significance by describing how Mayhew 'travels into the poor man's country for us' and on his return brings

> A picture of human life so wonderful, so awful, so piteous and pathetic, so exciting and terrible, that readers of romances own they never read anything like to it … these wonders and terrors have been lying by your door and mine ever since we had a door of our own. We had but to go a hundred yards off and see for ourselves, but we never did.

What united *Boz* and Mayhew was a 'gastronomy of the eye' that classified the new social roles and characters of the metropolis.

At one end of the social spectrum, authors evoked sympathy for each carefully delineated 'type' of poverty; at the other end, they defined the appearance and ethic of the true gentleman and lady. How, these authors asked, could a discerning viewer distinguish a genuinely respectable professional (in medicine or law) from the clerks and pen-pushers who occupied the fringes of gentility, struggling to maintain or elevate their social position? In articles such as 'People One Doesn't Care to Meet', the journalists of the 1870s and 80s offered detailed descriptions of the 'cad', 'swell', or 'masher' who 'during the week is content to appear in the seediest and most threadbare garments, but on Sundays emerges in all the glories of gaiters, "masher" collars and a crutch stick'.

This was a gendered discourse. It served a particularly powerful function in attempting to distinguish the prostitutes present at every society event from the respectable women around them. The latter were rendered natural and effortless in their grace, while the prostitute was an inauthentic try-hard: 'mark how she struts and stalks along, thinking that she is gracing the room with an elegant and refined style of locomotion'. Fear concerning prostitution, 'the great sin of great cities', remained a crucial element in the construction of these 'living panoramas' of urban life. From Charles Lamb's 1802 description of 'London-with-the-many-sins … City abounding in whores', to Pre-Raphaelite paintings of 'fallen women' to the vision of the prostitute in George Bernard Shaw's *Mrs Warren's Profession* (1894), hundreds of sources attest to efforts to comprehend the roles of prostitution in the respectable city.

This visual vocabulary of 'authenticity' and respectability was an informal sociological guide, operating in parallel to a new (Europe-wide) emphasis on statistical investigation and urban mapping to help the middle classes maintain some grip while the social structure changed so rapidly that old status markers no longer held.

KEY TEXTS OF THE SOCIAL OBSERVERS

Most of these factual descriptions of urban poverty were produced in the socio-economic crises of the 1840s or the closing decades of the century.

- Edwin Chadwick, *The Sanitary Condition of the Labouring Population* (1842)
- Friedrich Engels, *The Condition of the Working Classes in England* (1844)
- Henry Mayhew, *London Labour and the London Poor* (1851)
- Josephine Butler, *The Education and Employment of Women* (1868)
- Andrew Mearns, *The Bitter Cry of Outcast London* (1883)
- Charles Booth, *Life and Labour of the People in London* (1891–1903)
- Jack London, *The People of the Abyss* (1903)

The list of characteristics the *London Daily News* attributed to Jack London's book – 'tortured phrase, vehemence of denunciation, splashes of colour, and ferocity of epithet' – could have been applied to many of the others.

By the time they were collected in 1851, Mayhew's journalistic essays were not isolated instances of social exploration. The genre of 'social problem novel' and a whole range of texts bemoaning 'the condition of England' had begun to focus middle-class attention on questions of inequality, deprivation, and disease. The middle and upper classes had long been in denial about the horrors in their midst, but the early Victorian period (roughly speaking, the years between *Boz* in 1836 and *London Labour* in 1851) can be seen as the great moment of awakening. A huge project of urban analysis by the Benthamite social reformer Edwin Chadwick had been published as a *Report on the Sanitary Condition of the Labouring Population* (1842): this helped instigate what has been called 'the sanitary moment'. Through horrific statistics concerning life expectancy in inner cities and vivid explanations of the root causes of such problems, Chadwick's work revealed the urgency of improving water supply and drainage.

Another powerful symptom of the awakening of elites to urban horrors was a 'condition of England' novel penned by an individual who would later become one of the most powerful political leaders of the century, the twice-serving Prime Minister Benjamin Disraeli. This was entitled *Sybil, Or the Two Nations* (1845). *Sybil* was populated by wealthy aristocrats who refused to recognize the scale of social inequality and by political radicals who argued that British labourers were 'the most miserable people on the face of the globe': in living within view of extravagant wealth, they 'are not only degraded but conscious of their degradation'. As the social historian E.P. Thompson wrote, 'people may consume more goods and become less happy or less free at the same time', suffering 'intensified exploitation, greater insecurity, and increasing human misery'. This was what seemed to have happened, even for many Londoners who were not destitute and deprived, in the decade soon labelled 'the hungry forties'. Disraeli portrayed a London in which the two nations of the novel's title – the rich and the poor – were entirely separate entities with nothing but geography in common.

By the mid-Victorian period, one distinctive product of this urban crisis was a phenomenon that would change how city dwellers experience urban space forever: suburbanization. The horrors of the inner city created the desirability of commuting and gave impetus to the transport initiatives that still shape London life. The most characteristic was the London underground. The first line opened in January 1863 and in its first year alone carried ten million passengers between Paddington and Farringdon. Five years later, this 'Metropolitan Line' was complemented by a 'District Line' between South Kensington and Westminster. The Circle Line was added in 1884 and by 1900 deeper lines were being excavated as provision reached further and further into suburban satellites.

Despite perpetuating the tradition of first-, second-, and third-class carriages, the underground was intended as a democratic enterprise, assisting not just the middle classes, but also working people, in the flight from inner-city slums. However, the tube did not succeed in preventing the early years of suburbanization from being dominated by the middle classes. In fact, when the 'respectable' left city centres each evening, it seemed they had abandoned the streets to vice and corruption. Suburbanization, according to journalists at the time, accelerated the moral collapse of urban life: it permitted hordes of drunken revellers, engaged in 'ribald jesting' and even more profane antics, to run riot in otherwise empty streets. Only in the last third of the century, when real wages finally began to rise for poorer labourers, did suburbanization become a significant working-class phenomenon; it took further legislation, including the 1883 Cheap Trains Act (which provided reduced fares for workmen in the early morning and evening), for the underground to become a viable option for the poor.

Suburbs, however, were not yet the stuff of literature or reportage: they did not inspire sensory extravaganzas in prose, art, or verse. Central London in the 1880s and 90s was still a major destination for the chronicler of cities. This was a moment characterized by the birth of Aesthetic and Decadent movements associated with the names of Oscar Wilde and Aubrey Beardsley;

movements that challenged the prevalent Victorian idea that morality should be the primary lens through which all things should be viewed. The city itself need no longer be the 'good' city of progress and invention or the 'evil' city of vice and poverty, but could be a morally ambiguous city 'beyond good and evil' to be appreciated for its novel aesthetic power: even corruption could be beautiful.

Among the many visitors to embrace that attitude was the novelist Henry James, who arrived in London in 1876. The streets he described were not pleasant or 'agreeable, or cheerful, or easy … only magnificent'. It was ironic, he noted, that the great capital of a world empire should also be that empire's worst organized city. 'London is so clumsy and brutal, and has gathered together so many of the darkest sides of life' that it would be 'frivolous to ignore' the deformities of this 'strangely mingled monster': an 'ogress who devours human flesh … to do her tremendous work'. As this makes clear, James was intensely aware of London's problems. In a typically late nineteenth-century mode, he did not recoil from these horrors but embraced them: 'the impression of suffering was part of the general vibration'. He experienced unprecedented freedom and pleasure in the midst of the dangerous, disjointed city. 'I had complete liberty … I took possession of London; I felt it to be the right place.'

This disconnection and moral neutrality went far beyond anything expressed by Boz. It was a characteristic product of the end of the Victorian period, when a new consensus had emerged that life in the metropolis was a unique, path-breaking phenomenon. The psychology of the modern city was now analysed as a new development in the human condition. It was exciting rather than (or as well as) being terrifying.

The most subtle analyst of the new urban condition, the social theorist Georg Simmel, wrote his classic study of this theme, 'The Metropolis and Mental Life', in Dresden in 1903. He argued that the essence of the urban psyche was heightened sensory awareness, stimulated by the new tempo of day-to-day life and rapid, unprecedented, changes in social environment. 'The rapid crowding of changing images, the sharp discontinuity in the grasp of a single glance, and the unexpectedness of onrushing impressions' had led, in the late nineteenth century, to an entirely new psychology.

This newly aestheticized space was the *City of Dreadful Delight* described by the cultural historian Judith Walkowitz in her 1992 study of late Victorian society. Old traditions of power and control, Walkowitz demonstrates, were undermined by the new order on the city's streets. New kinds of sexuality, new interpretations of class, new sensational mass journalism, and new urban freedoms made the city 'modern' in the late Victorian decades.

A hanging

Victorian public hangings provide a remarkable instance of the spectacle of London's streets. It was not just in the 1890s that the very worst of the city's faults, the greatest fears lurking in the shadows, were a source of macabre entertainment. As scholars including Rosalind Crone, Sarah Waters, and Judith Flanders have shown, early Victorian murderers could gain extraordinary celebrity. Alongside this, the retributive justice of the gallows became a heavily commercialized public event. Investigating these themes can help us understand the rapidly changing culture of the Victorian city.

PUBLIC EXECUTIONS AND LEGAL CHANGE

Mass urbanization led to social disorder on a large scale. Early nineteenth-century authorities had few resources to deal with this. Because catching a large proportion of criminals was impossible, the favoured deterrent was a penal code of extravagant severity. Almost two hundred offences were subject to hanging or transportation to penal colonies. These ranged from stealing anything worth more than five shillings to spending a month in the company of gypsies or walking the streets after dark with a blackened face. In the early nineteenth century, over a thousand men and women a year were sentenced to death (although many eventually escaped execution).

In 1829, Robert Peel's Metropolitan Police Act established a police force in London. Over the following decades, this innovation spread to other urban centres: by 1848, only 22 of 171 English boroughs did not have a police force. The advent of effective policing was accompanied by a relaxation of the penal code. This was a gradual process, which focused the heaviest punishments on violent crime and treason. In the year Victoria came to the throne, arson and burglary were removed from the list of crimes punishable by death. In the previous five years, sheep, cattle, and horse stealing had been removed, as had sacrilege, letter stealing, and forgery. In 1865, only five crimes remained capital offences. These developments contributed to the Victorians' belief that they had a civilized society, making it a more humane and caring place that fitted their religious values and political convictions.

The joint hangings of husband and wife Frederick and Maria Manning, whose crimes were known as the 'Bermondsey Horror', took place at Horsemonger Lane Gaol in 1849. Because it was the first joint execution of a husband and wife for over a century, the event aroused phenomenal public interest, drawing a crowd of over 40,000 spectators. The crime they were hanged for was one of passion: the murder of Maria's lover, Patrick O'Connor, whom they had not only shot but also bludgeoned with a crowbar. To increase visibility and indulge the crowds, the hanging took place on a rooftop and owners of nearby homes found that they could make 'at minimum a year's rent by simply letting out rooms with the view'.

One of the spellbound crowd on this occasion was Charles Dickens, already a prominent voice in heated debates over capital punishment. He soon immortalized Maria Manning, a Swiss-born domestic servant, as Mademoiselle Hortense, Lady Dedlock's maid in *Bleak House*. But Dickens was present to observe the immense crowd as much as to judge the punishment itself. He had become fascinated by the idea of isolation amidst crowds and mused on the extraordinary tension they generated between fear of bodily contagion and hope for human connection. On this occasion, he was in a pessimistic mood, as he wrote to *The Times*:

> I believe that a sight so inconceivably awful as the wickedness and levity of the immense crowd collected at that execution this morning could be imagined by no man, and could be presented in no heathen land under the sun.

Like society at large, the legal system in the early nineteenth century had undergone what the social theorist Norbert Elias christened a 'civilising process'. As a result, the number of executions had fallen dramatically from the days of the eighteenth-century 'Bloody Code' when hanging could be administered for even minor felonies.

Yet, as Vic Gatrell's book *The Hanging Tree* showed, this had side effects. Each individual execution now received more attention than ever before. State authorities had deliberately worked to make hangings more theatrical. They introduced a 'New Drop' that killed cleanly (thereby reducing the likelihood that observers would sympathize with the hanged), and they carefully stage-managed the main arena for hangings at Newgate Prison. This was all calculated to maximize each execution's cautionary power. The result was what the historian Simon Deveraux calls a 'newly revivified drama of deterrence' in which all of society took a role as either spectator or performer. (The online database of the Old Bailey Online is a wonderful resource for those who wish to be audience to this drama.)

One of the most astonishing features of these dramatized occasions was their commercial spinoffs, the range of which is indicative of the vibrancy of street culture. They included 'broadsides' which were the equivalent of a theatre programme, thousands of which can now be viewed online via the John Johnson collection or the British Library. Broadsides packed together as much diverse information as possible on a single large sheet of paper. This ranged from the most gory details of the crime itself, to sensationalized accounts of the lives of victim and perpetrator, with the former typically made to conform to all Victorian ideals, while the latter's life was elaborated to flout all conventions of gender, class, and religious propriety. There were often accounts, usually fabricated, of the last, contrite, words of the condemned:

> Good people, you have now come to see an unfortunate woman die, let my situation be a warning to you all, and young women avoid jealousy, for that caused me to commit the horrid crime of murder.

Sometimes broadsides went even further in consolidating this message, offering explicit accounts of the 'moral' to be drawn from such an event:

> Indulge not thyself in the passion of anger; it is whetting a sword to wound thine own breast, or murder thy friend. Harbour not revenge in thy breast, it will torment thy heart, and discolour its best inclinations. Read this to your children and preserve it.

These sheets were sold by noisy hawkers who populated street corners and filled thoroughfares with vocal sales pitches. Their wares were intended as mementos, but also to convey information to those not present at the event. It is estimated that two and a half million broadsides were printed relating to the execution of the Mannings. No other kind of text – not novel or newspaper – could hope to rival this scale of sales. This form of textual persuasion proved phenomenally successful. After riots at the execution for forgery of Ann Hurle in 1804, and the strange debacle of Robert Johnston, hanged four times for robbing an Edinburgh candlemaker in 1818 (various errors, such as a short length of rope, allowed the twenty-two-year-old to survive the first three attempts to hang him: the outraged crowd stormed the gallows and threw Johnston's coffin through a church window), there is not a single instance of London crowds expressing discontent at an execution they saw as unjust: the moral message of the broadsides was more powerful than any legislative act.

From the backstreet printer of broadsides or the street-corner crier selling them by the cartload, to the establishment executioner and his adjuncts, all were part of the society of the spectacle. If Queen Victoria, under whose authority these executions were conducted, was 'the first media monarch' (as John Plunkett's 2003 biography of her suggested), then the Victorian hanging was brutal justice for the media age. Hangings had come to occupy a space between entertainment and moral lesson. This can be seen in the many strange celebrations of the events that can be found in popular culture, parodied here in 1849 verses from *Punch* entitled 'The Great Moral Lesson at Horsemonger Lane Gaol':

> Hurrah! you dogs, for hangin, the feelins to excite;
> I could ha throttled BILL almost, that moment, with delight.
> But, arter all, what is it? A tumble and a kick!
> And, anyhow, tis seemingly all over precious quick,
> And shows that some, no matter for what they've done, dies game!
> Ho, ho! if ever my time comes, I hope to do the same!

The rise of the public

Murder, hanging, and even fraud were not just commemorated in broadsides, but had all kinds of commercial forms built around them. Stage plays, melodramas, puppet shows, and even Staffordshire earthenware pottery were among a vast array of genres used to commemorate any particularly gruesome event.

Between the 1830s and the 1850s, restrictions on commercial activity, including taxes on paper and state control of the press, fell away at extraordinary speed as many forms of authority were transferred from the state to the public. This can be understood as a late stage in the emergence of a 'public sphere', a concept developed by the German theorist Jurgen Habermas and adapted by historians such as Tim Blanning to elucidate aspects of the social history of the eighteenth and nineteenth centuries. The public sphere was a direct product of urbanization, made possible when large numbers of middle- or upper-working-class people with common interests were brought together. This concentration of co-operating individuals could pool their growing resources, which allowed the moderately well-off to rival the economic power of landed aristocrats. They could create cultural forms that were not centralized, official, or state-sanctioned but emerged directly from the marketplace and catered to public demand.

As Tim Blanning has shown, music offers one of the clearest demonstrations of the workings of this public sphere. Composers in the seventeenth and early eighteenth centuries wrote not for the public, but for private patrons. The works of J.S. Bach or G.F. Handel were commissioned by royal, religious, or aristocratic patrons and the music they composed reflected the grandeur of the church or the regal self-image of the wealthy sponsor. Ticketed concerts, patronized by the middle classes as well as the aristocracy, were an eighteenth-century innovation made possible by the public sphere, which transformed the prospects of composers. Josef Haydn and W.A. Mozart began their careers in traditional servile status, but by the end of the century took advantage of opportunities that had not been available to Bach. They were able to pursue parallel careers as celebrities who composed and performed for paying metropolitan crowds. London and Paris, as the largest and wealthiest cities in Europe, provided the audiences that could yield the greatest riches. A host of Victorian-era composers took advantage of the status of international celebrity, including Franz Liszt, 'the Byron of the piano', who toured his extravagant, theatrical performances around Britain in the 1840s and 1880s.

This change transformed musical style. The unified moods of royal works such as Handel's *Zadok the Priest*, composed for the coronation of George II, were intended to convey the pomp and grandeur of the office of king (an ideal known as 'Unity of Affekt'). These gave way to the argumentative structures of the classical symphony and sonata, in which the first movement was always driven by stark contrasts between conflicting musical themes. Such musical strife was ill suited to direct expression of power, but was an artistic counterpart to the public sphere's encouragement of democratic public debate.

This shift of power from patron to audience, and from landed wealth to commercial culture, had further implications. It created the space in which new roles such as impresario, advertiser, and music critic were born. Ever more public events competed for audiences, and these audiences grew increasingly educated and discerning. Urban streets were marked by these developments as billboard advertising became more competitive and extensive. Competition also encouraged the emergence of new authorities who made a living from guiding public taste. Publications multiplied. These featured everything from reviews of concerts or biographies of composers to idealized pictures of performers. Piano transcriptions of orchestral works were published so that the latest pieces could be performed in the privacy of the bourgeois home. New inexpensive pianos made the instrument a symbol of middle-class status.

During this period, the role of the British public in the musical life of Europe increased. Leading composers from the German states, such as Felix Mendelssohn and Richard Wagner, made their way to London (and often to Birmingham and Manchester too) as a rite of passage. From Mendelssohn's *Elijah* (1844) and second piano concerto, to Dvorak's *Stabat Mater* (1877), many of the great international works of the period were composed for British cities, and a work like *Elijah* could become a lasting symbol of civic pride for an aspirational city such as Birmingham.

The public sphere was inseparable from a vast expansion in print culture, which allowed the Victorians to read more than anyone before them. This reading also covered more topics than ever. It was because everything that could be imagined could now be set down in print that the Victorians did not consider writing about music to be like 'dancing about architecture'. The founders of lending libraries aimed to ensure that this cult of reading was not just a middle-class pursuit but reached those with less disposable income. Cheap ventures such as the *Penny Magazine* (1832–45) were part of a missionary effort to empower the poor through print. The works of Dickens and his peers were published in instalments, often as features in periodicals, so that the cost of purchase could be spread over several months.

Books, pamphlets, and periodicals were central to a vast new range of public spaces, which shaped the urban landscape. The welcoming architecture of the lending library could be found nestled amidst printing shops, bookshops, mechanics' institutes, literary and philosophical societies, gentlemen's clubs, coffee houses, and the reading rooms of societies and trade bodies that had been founded to promote all kinds of pursuits.

RATIONAL RECREATION

In the mid-Victorian period in particular, the middle classes encouraged specific forms of leisure that they felt would discourage radicalism, labour unrest, and bad health. Leisure, they argued, should be both respectable and productive. Moralizers were suspicious of existing entertainment, so, in the cultural historian Peter Bailey's words, sought to devise 'suitably brisk and purposeful recreations'. They developed athletics as a respectable alternative to boxing or blood sports. Sports such as football and tennis were codified and institutionalized: they ceased to be free-for-alls and became respectable pursuits that encouraged discipline, self-control, teamwork, and physical vigour. Wimbledon Lawn Tennis and Croquet Club emerged in this way. Aston Villa and Everton football clubs grew out of Methodist chapels, while Sunderland football club was a collaborative venture started by the town's teachers. Swimming baths were built in many towns, usually funded by middle-class philanthropy. Taking sea air became a Victorian obsession, leading to the transformation into holiday resorts of a host of seaside towns, from Blackpool to Brighton.

This was all part of an effort to moralize urban space. Drawing on the heavenly vision of the New Jerusalem, Christianity was increasingly conceptualized as 'the religion of Cities'. Churches and Sunday Schools, like libraries, were among the forms of architecture to proliferate most dramatically. Other educational institutions were not far behind. Public parks and baths were constructed as spaces for 'rational recreation'. This idea could seem to be a panacea: healthier leisure pursuits seemed to promise that the next generation would be more robust, creative, thrifty, and virtuous than their predecessors. However, amidst the largely uncontrolled growth of diverse entertainment, this effort to 'rationalize' recreation was not necessarily a battle that middle-class moralizers could win.

Music hall

The tension between morality and entertainment is perhaps seen more clearly in the songs and comic turns of the music hall stage than in the opera house or concert hall. Music hall is now, thanks to one historian in particular, a well-trodden field of Victorian history. Peter Bailey has drawn such riches from analysis of the performance of both singers and audiences in popular theatres that his work has expanded conceptions of what Victorian history is, making it possible to see new significance in diverse aspects of Victorian experience. Music hall has ceased to be something that merely evokes rose-tinted visions of the 'good old days' and has become a crucial site for analysis of social and cultural transformation.

The music hall was a particularly democratic product of the public sphere described above. The expansion of urban public spaces in the 1830s and 40s gave rise to a phenomenal range of new forms of leisure. This was, for instance, the first great age of the modern circus. Such expansion was possible because, although the very poor were mired in horrific conditions, there were many others with slowly increasing real wages and leisure time. As the century went on, the number who could spare some resources for entertainment expanded and makeshift forms of recreation – whether sport or the arts – were slowly commercialized. Yet leisure was still considered a 'problem'. The fear generated by the French Revolution, the economic crises of the Napoleonic Wars, and the harsh strictures of early Victorian religion had all combined to create lasting prejudice against entertainment and to give the early Victorians a reputation for unyielding seriousness.

Even Henry Mayhew was fiercely critical of the role of leisure and music hall in the lives of the poor. Like many other such accounts, his descriptions derived their horror from suggesting that the poor were transgressing traditional boundaries. He responds with shock when children behave like adults or when working people mimic gentlemen or ladies. The prevalence of these transgressions meant that working-class leisure seemed to threaten the social order. Mayhew insisted that

> It is impossible to contemplate the ignorance and immorality of … coster-mongers [fruit and vegetable sellers], without

> wishing to discover the cause of their degradation. Let anyone curious on this point visit one of these penny shows … the stage, instead of being the means for illustrating a moral precept, is turned into a platform to teach the cruelest debauchery. The audience is usually composed of children so young, that these dens become the school-rooms where the guiding morals of a life are picked up, and so precocious are the little things, that the girl of nine will, from constant attendance at such places, have learnt to understand the filthiest sayings, and laugh at them as loudly as the grown-up lads around her … Some of the girls – though their figures showed them to be mere children – were dressed in showy cotton-velvet polkas, and wore dowdy feathers in their crushed bonnets. They stood laughing and joking with the lads, in an unconcerned, impudent manner that was almost appalling. Some of them, when tired of waiting, chose their partners, and commenced dancing grotesquely, to the admiration of the lookers-on, who expressed their approbation in obscene terms, that, far from disgusting the poor little women, were received as compliments, and acknowledged with smiles and coarse repartees.

Throughout the century, tensions between pleasure seekers ('devotees of gin, beer, and fun') and moralizers ('heirs of the puritans') persisted and only as political and economic conditions mellowed after 1850 did the latter lose their upper hand. By the 1860s, the *Saturday Review* could record a new 'habit of enjoyment', which gave birth to 'an axiom with many young people that they have a right to be always amused, or to be always going to be amused'; looking back at the 1830s from 1884, Walter Besant, the historian and 'social topographer', enjoined his readers to 'remember how very little play went on even among the comfortable and opulent classes in those days … dullness and a serious view of life seemed inseparable'. This portrait of early Victorian Britain as a land without leisure was part myth, but also part genuine memory of a society that had been in crisis.

Through all this, the rise of music hall gathered pace. At the beginning of the Victorian period, the entertainment made to cater for urban crowds was small scale and improvised, taking place in roadside public houses. Soon, the regular singsongs or occasional comic turns of the tavern back room developed into more specialized forms of leisure. Relaxation of legal strictures on stage performance ended the monopolies possessed by a handful of expensive official playhouses. This allowed the emergence of dozens of popular theatres. At the same time, the back-room singsong was slowly professionalized, with performers able to earn a healthy living as well as considerable celebrity. Soon there were hundreds of dedicated music halls across Britain, and over thirty in London alone. Paid performers would circulate between these halls, performing the same 'turns' several times each evening.

These venues were dismissed as vulgar and rowdy by middle-class educators and social commentators: drinking through performances was the norm, while the presence of prostitutes and their clients consolidated associations between the popular stage and public vice. But audiences were not just made up of the rowdier elements of the working class. As the form commercialized, music hall became a key venue to observe the classes mingling and at play. By the 1890s, over 45,000 people of all classes were crowding into London music halls every night.

More significantly still, music hall became a forum in which Victorian society made sense of itself. As Peter Bailey has demonstrated, the repertoire of the halls was full of commentary on the quirks of class. This facilitates what many social historians have considered their 'holy grail': a vision of the urban social structure from the perspective not of wealthy authors but of the working classes themselves. Performers played the part of chimney sweeps facing the gallows, or of upper-class toffs and swells. They drew humour from situations of class confusion, such as the behaviour of newly wealthy labourers who guzzled champagne despite their cockney accents.

Bailey's sophisticated studies of this phenomenon include essays on gender, such as 'Musical comedy and the rhetoric of the girl' and 'The Victorian barmaid as cultural prototype', as well as studies of class and status as performed categories, including 'Champagne Charlie and the Music-Hall Swell Song' and 'Will the Real Bill Banks Please Stand Up? A Role Analysis of Working-Class Respectability'. These essays on music hall and popular culture are now part of a vast and subtle literature exploring the late Victorian city. The sexuality of the streets is elucidated by Judith Walkowitz; middle-class fascination with poverty is explored by Seth Koven; urban space is analysed by Simon Gunn; department stores and consumption are interpreted by Erika Rappaport and Deborah Cohen. These works convey the complex, intricate ways in which mutations in the social order redefined the public and private spaces of the modern city. More importantly, readers of these historians discover how these changes were negotiated, explained, and manipulated by those who occupied the slums, streets, promenades, or palaces of Victorian London. London, however, was a unique phenomenon. It was not just different from other world cities, but also distinct from the wildly diverse settlements around the rest of Britain.

3

Knowing Victorian Britain: the geography of four nations

The Gaelic language may be what it likes, both as to antiquity and beauty, but it decidedly stands in the way of the civilization of the natives making use of it, and shuts them out from the paths open to their fellow-countrymen who speak the English tongue. It ought, therefore, to cease to be taught in all our national schools; and as we are one people we should have but ONE language.

Registrar General's Report (1871)

No nineteenth-century nation was united. Many peasants in rural France were unaware that they were French (so much so that a historical work by Eugen Weber entitled *Peasants into Frenchmen* covered only the period after 1870). Politicians, artists, and intellectuals in small states such as Saxony or Sardinia committed great effort to inventing the idea of Germany or Italy before those nations, in the 1870s, became political realities. The United Kingdom of Great Britain and Ireland was another new entity, created by the Acts of Union in 1801. Britain itself was not much older: an eighteenth-century invention. In all these new nations, when words for 'unity' were thrown around (as they constantly were), they were usually a smokescreen: they obscured the extent of diversity in cultures that were never genuinely 'national'.

To make any real sense of the new world the Victorians made, we will need to look far beyond London. Even more than today, the metropolis was only a tiny fraction of the world British people inhabited, and it was a particularly odd one. London's economy, culture, and politics were irreconcilably different from circumstances elsewhere in the Victorians' sphere of activity. We will need to explore the forces that worked to increase the distance between London and Lerwick, Galway and Great Yarmouth, or even Manitoba and Melbourne, as well as those (such as steam-powered transport) that fostered unprecedented integration. This will mean dealing not just with the period 1837–1901, but also the preceding four decades. These were the years in which the shape of Victorian Britain was established. This was also the era in which new kinds of national and regional identity were formed.

The first step for nineteenth-century politicians marvelling at their nation's diversity was to attempt to record it on paper. Mapping was a Victorian love affair, and in indulging it the Victorians proved themselves extraordinarily proficient geographers. The institution that mapped Britain, the Ordnance Survey, was founded in 1791 and soon became one of Britain's most esteemed scientific bodies. Between the 1790s and 1860s, the Survey created the first comprehensive, detailed map of Britain. In the following decades, the advent of the bicycle gave cartographers a new flexibility. As this suggests, the Ordnance Survey operated in a world that now looks remarkably low-tech. But its ambitions were exhaustive and imperious. It is no coincidence that the first national map the Ordnance Survey completed was that of Ireland: a nation that was essentially colonized. This was the part of the British Isles where people most successfully resisted the coercion to identify with the concept of 'Britishness' and this had also been the first region of Britain to receive a state-organized police force (1814). The Victorians understood the close connection between mapping and the pursuit of control in contested places. They were well aware, in other words, of the relationship between knowledge and power.

Mapping, however, was only one aspect of an intensifying endeavour to know what, in terms of people, cultures, and landscapes, the British Isles contained. In the peace that followed the vast overspending of the Napoleonic Wars, the government needed to build Britain into an efficient, taxable entity. Yet most London-based officials knew little about Britain beyond the commercial South East. National censuses, introduced in 1801, had been an attempt to overcome this insularity, but these were at an early stage of development: even after the first census there was confusion about such fundamental things as whether the population of Britain was expanding or contracting.

The task of knowing Britain was made more urgent by a radically shifting balance of power. Many regions of England's north and west, particularly new industrial centres such as Manchester, were booming. These emerging cities sapped the population of struggling rural areas, becoming manufacturing conurbations of unprecedented productive power: London's statisticians and politicians were forced to think in a new national frame. The founding of the Statistical Society of London (1834) symbolized this realization of the early 1830s.

There was not even any well-established language for talking about Britain's multiple levels of geographical organization: region, nation, and union were rarely discussed with precision. Throughout the century, the English often failed to differentiate between 'England' and 'Britain': they frequently treated Wales, Ireland, and Scotland as hazy Celtic hinterlands lost in the mist of time. Even Dickens's geography was shaky. In *Hard Times*, Mrs Sparsit makes improbably rapid journeys between towns such as Liverpool and Manchester because her creator, born in Portsmouth and raised in London, substantially underestimated the scale of Northern England. When another leading (though now neglected) novelist, Mary Ward, listed 'the great English religious thinkers', there were Scots as well as Englishmen on her list.

POPULATION

- The different fate of each region is demonstrated by population changes across the Victorian period.
- In 1837, the population of the United Kingdom was 25.5 million; by 1901 it grew to 41 million (an increase of 61%).
- The population of England rose most rapidly: from 15 million to 32.3 million (increase of 116%).
- In contrast, the population of Ireland decreased from 8 million to 4.5 million (decrease of 44%).
- The result was that where the Irish population had made up 31% of the population of Britain in 1837 it accounted for just 9% in 1901.

Scotland and Ireland did at least receive substantial official attention (although much of it was hostile and unwelcome). Britishness was often thought of as the 'blending' of Scottish and English characteristics, and Parliament devoted intense focus to the 'Irish question'. In these circumstances, it was Wales that was most consistently sidelined by overweening Englishness. Welsh-language culture was, and is, one of the most vibrant phenomena in Britain, yet most Victorians considered it an irrelevant enclave or a pernicious barrier to progress. Queen Victoria, more ostentatiously 'British' than any monarch before her, is estimated to have spent seven years of her reign in Scotland, seven weeks in Ireland but only seven days in Wales. More telling still is the entry for Wales in a nineteenth-century edition of the *Encyclopaedia Britannica*: 'For Wales, see England'. To many English people, political union between the nations and regions of Britain seemed to mean little more than assimilation of 'provinces' into metropolitan English culture.

The four nations from Union (1801) to reform (1832)

The United Kingdom of Great Britain and Ireland existed for only a little longer than the Victorian period. Established in 1801 with the Acts of Union, it ended in 1922 with the establishment of the Irish Free State. This was the only period in history when the British Isles have been a single political entity. Between these dates, Parliament committed immense resources to try to sustain this coherence, but the condition of the Union remained a cause of constant worry. The effort to protect a political settlement that brought together diverse cultures, including several different languages, took up vast amounts of time for Victorian parliamentarians and became the dominating issue of several political careers.

The 1801 Acts of Union form a crucial backdrop to Victorian debates. These were primarily security measures, rushed through Parliament amidst fears that Ireland might side with France in war against Britain. The Irish lost their independent parliament but gained representation in London. However, the application of these Acts was far more problematic and oppressive than their original conception had been. The Prime Minister who passed the Acts, William Pitt, had intended to secure religious freedoms for Irish Catholics, yet King George III refused and in so doing ensured the continuation of officially sanctioned anti-Catholic discrimination. Pitt resigned in protest, but in George III's exercise of royal prerogative the tensions that bedevilled the Anglo–Irish relationship for the whole Victorian period (and far beyond) had been established.

From 1801, Parliament housed 489 English MPs, 24 Welsh, 45 Scottish and 100 Irish (all Protestant). Only in 1829 was a Catholic emancipation bill finally introduced, allowing Catholics to sit in Parliament; however, this was also a measure of control that, among other things, drastically reduced the Irish electorate.

The following years saw a degree of reform to the electoral system, including the Great Reform Act (1832). However, those entitled to vote in England only increased from 400,000 to 650,000 in a population of 14 million.

Furthermore, reform did not substantially alter the imbalance between the four nations. In the 1820s, England accounted for approximately half the British population, yet contained three-quarters of those eligible to vote (fewer than 5,000 Scots were enfranchised). Before reform, England contained 74% of voters; reform only reduced this figure to 71%. The parliamentary establishment had particular reasons for maintaining this balance: where England remained the heartland of conservative politics, Scotland, Ireland, and Wales showed much more radical inclinations.

The contradiction between the importance of the Celtic nations and their enforced marginality can be seen most clearly in their relationship to empire. The Scots, Irish, and Welsh were mainstays of Empire, administrating and fighting for the imperial establishment. They dominated some fields of British politics (some late Victorian commentators even liked to suggest that the English were the marginalized faction in the Union). However, twenty-first-century books and articles with titles like *Postcolonial Wales* or 'Ireland and Postcolonial Theory' recognize that the Celtic nations shared some experiences with oppressed colonies of the British Empire. Reacting against triumphalism concerning the industrial revolution, these books and articles point out that British economic growth was not a universal benefit even within Britain: it had grisly effects for Ireland as well as India and parts of Africa.

Far more successful in fostering a Victorian sense of unity, however, were the careers of several leading Victorian sages and statesmen. By the mid-Victorian period, many public figures, including four-times Prime Minister William Gladstone, were emphatically British rather than English.

WILLIAM EWART GLADSTONE (1809–98)

Gladstone had a long and distinguished career in politics, serving four times as Liberal Prime Minister. This career was not narrowly English, but expansively British. Born into a prominent Scottish family, Gladstone was brought up in Liverpool. He forged alliances with many of the Northern manufacturers, such as the Rochdale carpet maker John Bright, who campaigned for better political representation of interests of Northern cities. Gladstone married into a Welsh family and lived in North Wales (Hawarden) where he found many committed supporters. From his disestablishment of the Church of Ireland in his first period as Prime Minister (1868–74) to his efforts to secure Irish Home Rule in his third ministry (1886), much of Gladstone's career was spent attempting to mitigate the problems the English Parliament had imposed on Ireland. Despite all this, Gladstone, in common with most parliamentarians, used the phrase 'the English' to refer to all inhabitants of mainland Britain.

Britishness has been an important topic of debate in recent historiography. The most influential author on this theme is Linda Colley, whose book *Britons: Forging the Nation* argued that, despite the tensions generated by the Union, the decades around 1801 were crucial in generating a coherent ideal of British identity. This, she insists, was formed around three forces: wartime patriotism directed against France, Protestantism, and the shared role of the four nations in wielding imperial power. Perhaps less exciting but at least as rich in historical detail, Keith Robbins's *Nineteenth-Century Britain: Integration and Diversity* extends analysis of these themes into the Victorian period.

Robbins shows how, despite their conceptual and geographical fuzziness, the Victorians had new reasons to take the geography of Britain seriously. As the economy developed and cities grew, migration around Britain increased rapidly (of city dwellers in 1851, only a third had been born in the city that was their home). From the 1830s, a new technology – railways with steam locomotives – facilitated rapid travel, which became crucial to the reordering of Britain. It created, for instance, the potential for national working-class political movements: by the 1840s, the champions of anti-establishment claims for full democratic representation travelled between radical centres such as Newcastle, Leeds, and Manchester to address large crowds of discontented workers.

The industrial revolution and the rise of a national radical politics were accompanied by the increasing integration of Britain as an economic system, but this did not mean an increasingly homogenous nation. Instead, different regions could fulfil distinctive purposes within an increasingly national frame. The identities of Manchester or Belfast as industrial centres, Leith or Liverpool as port towns, and Newcastle or Blaenafon as mining centres grew increasingly distinctive and self-confident after 1837. Each became the focal point of its own larger industrial sphere. These new regional ties redrew the map of Britain, ignoring national boundaries. For instance, the English counties of Herefordshire and Gloucestershire were drawn under the influence of the industrial centres of South Wales; at the same time, the Welsh counties of Fflint and Denbighshire became economic chattels to the industrial powerhouses of North West England. The possibility of a 'British' culture was increased at the same time as the distinctiveness and self-confidence of vibrant cultural centres such as Cardiff, Edinburgh, Kirkwall, and Bristol were consolidated.

British cityscapes are still deeply marked by these developments. The impressive civic buildings of towns such as Leeds, Nottingham, or Birmingham are products of this growing swagger: in the 1830s, town centres that had been slums were cleared and remade as impressive Victorian public spaces. As the urban historian Simon Gunn has shown, this was a reconceptualization of public space that created the modern city with its non-residential civic centre and its stratified suburbs. This rebuilding of city centres was often an expression of civic pride that usually stemmed from industry and commerce. The results could be eccentric. In Leeds, for example, Temple Works, the largest mill in the world, was given massive ancient Egyptian pillars and porticoes. This Victorian inventiveness was not confined to Britain. An elaborate new architectural style, known now as imperial gothic, soon marked the cityscapes of Calcutta and Melbourne with the same sentiments as defined the town centres of Bradford and Bedford. Localism, Britishness, and imperial transnationalism were apparent opposites, which were in fact always inseparable.

Whether in Calcutta or Cardiff these beautiful and unusual buildings were statements of civic ambition and products of rapidly changing ideas of what cities were and should be. All of them, however, were surrounded by narrow streets of squalid and undeveloped housing: the worlds of the well-to-do and the poverty-stricken seemed entirely unconnected, although separated by metres rather than miles. As Friedrich Engels put it, poverty 'dwells in hidden alleys, close to the palaces of the rich'. Removed from the view of the wealthy, who knew as little of slums as they did of the South Sea Isles, this degradation was nonetheless necessary to support their leisured existence. Understanding the nature of new urban spaces is a primary requirement for any student of the Victorians.

URBAN GROWTH IN NUMBERS

- Population of Britain's largest towns before the Victorian period:

1600	**1700**	**1800**
London 200,000	London 575,000	London 959,000
Norwich 15,000	Norwich 30,000	Manchester 89,000
York 12,000	Bristol 21,000	Liverpool 83,000

- Proportion of British people living in towns of over 10,000 people:

1800	**1850**	**1910**
23.1%	42.8%	71.3%

• Nineteenth-century populations

	1801	1861	1901
London	959,000	2,804,000	6,339,500
Manchester	90,000	338,300	543,900
Glasgow	77,000	395,500	762,000
Cardiff	6,300	49,000	172,600
Dublin	170,000	410,000	448,000

Literary cities: what did urbanization mean?

In 1960, Raymond Williams, one of the most influential scholars of Victorian culture, published a novel called *Border Country*. Its protagonist is a London lecturer in economic history who has spent his career analysing the transformation of English and Welsh geography in the Victorian period: he has charted, statistically, the move of millions from rural to urban life. However, he has become deeply disenchanted concerning the potential of facts and numbers to convey anything of value. What he seeks instead is the emotional and psychological impact of the new urban environments on those who had been born in a more traditional world of agricultural work. The novel's protagonist has himself moved from rural Wales (Glynmawr) to London and compares his own predicament with the experience of those he studies:

> He was working on population movements into the Welsh mining valleys in the middle decades of the nineteenth century. But I have moved myself, he objected, and what is it really that I must measure? The techniques I have learned have the solidity and precision of ice-cubes, while a given temperature is maintained. But it is a temperature I can't really maintain; the door of the box keeps flying

> open. It's hardly a population movement from Glynmawr to London, but it's a change of substance, as it must have been for them, when they left their villages. And the ways of measuring this are not only outside my discipline. They are somewhere else altogether, that I can feel but not handle, touch but not grasp. To the nearest hundred, or to any usable percentage, my single figure is indifferent, but it is the only relevant figure: without it, the change can't be measured at all.

This fictional character is concerned with a need to balance the large-scale aggregate overview with the psychologies of individual experience. Literature, as well as diaries, memoirs, and autobiography, provide psychological insight that statistics cannot.

This potential of literature and literary techniques to get under the skin of Victorian experience is celebrated in equally powerful terms by the literary scholar Philip Davis. Victorian literature, he insists, is usually about precisely the things we expect it to be. It does treat the topics of urbanization, industrialization, and the carving up of the landscape by roads and railway lines. It is about 'all those old words' that the sceptical 'might dismiss as humbug, which sound like cracked voices played out on worn-out records from great-grandfather's wind-up gramophone': 'Humanity, Duty, Vocation, Work, Marriage, Family'. However, the power of a George Eliot or Charles Dickens comes not from giving us new themes to think about, but from giving unexpected vitality and urgency to ideas that had previously seemed cobwebbed and mothballed:

> The great realist novelist takes those concerns to such a depth of living particularity that they no longer feel the same, whatever their public name. That is the sort of inner originality mostly on offer in Victorian literature: it is not entirely different from what you thought it was going

> to be about, it is just utterly redeemed from cliché by being in its true reality much more serious, much more important, much more complex and specific than you had ever supposed such ordinary things could be.

In no topic is this more true than in the changing human geography of Britain. Davis shows how writers such as Thomas Carlyle recognized that the challenges of the new city were not 'social problems'. They resisted any such neat categorization: 'they were mental, spiritual, emotional, cosmological even, as well as economic or political'. George Eliot's *Middlemarch*, Dickens's *Little Dorrit*, Charlotte Bronte's *Shirley*, and Elizabeth Gaskell's *North and South* each gives us a very different glimpse into the transformation of human experience that the new geographies could generate. A recent book edited by Keith Snell entitled *The Regional Novel in Britain and Ireland* demonstrates how far these fictional explorations of place extended beyond the Victorian canon.

ACTS OF ENCLOSURE AND THE 1815 CORN LAW

British agriculture was transformed in the eighteenth and early nineteenth centuries. Where 74% of the population had been employed in agricultural trades in 1700, only 35% were in 1800. At the beginning of the nineteenth century, small landholders and tenant farmers made up much of the rural population. Parliamentary enclosure was introduced region by region in the late eighteenth and early nineteenth centuries, consolidating small open fields into bigger 'enclosed' units. These were owned and controlled by large landowners who charged increasingly high rents. Enclosure was intended to rationalize agricultural production, overcoming the resistance of small farmers who refused to rotate crops or use other modern techniques. In the words of the socialist historian E.P. Thompson, this was 'a plain enough case of class robbery'. The question of whether enclosure increased productivity has been argued over at great length. What is certain is that, even if the phenomenon did have some economic benefits, it contributed only a tiny proportion of the improvement of agriculture between 1700 and 1850.

The Corn Law of 1815 (the last of a series of prohibitory laws stretching back to 1670) was in place until 1846. The Napoleonic Wars had led to high grain prices, which, in 1813, had begun to fall. The Corn Law aimed to curtail this decrease and has been presented as a 'naked piece of class legislation'. It was not, however, wholly unnecessary: agricultural expansion had led to the use of poor-quality land that could only possibly return profits if prices were high. However, the Corn Law did have similar class implications to enclosure. Its efforts to maintain high prices and land rents worked in the interests of property owners and against workers: it was labelled at the time 'a pact of famine' made between the government and the landed aristocracy.

Pressure to repeal the Corn Law arose quickly. The 1820s saw the popularization of an ideology of Free Trade, which suggested that all prices should exist at 'natural' levels rather than being artificially controlled. However, political disagreements over how to impose taxation and tackle a large national debt (incurred during the Napoleonic Wars) prevented consensus on reform of the Corn Law. Only after income tax was introduced in 1842 did the economy recover enough to run a budget surplus. In these improved circumstances, the advocates of Free Trade and the Anti-Corn Law League finally won their victory.

The experience of John Clare, the rural Northamptonshire poet, is as powerful as any of these novels. Clare's prose and poetry show us the effects of enforced mobility in a culture where tradition, memory, and local geographies played enormous roles. In poems like 'The Moores', he charts the psychological impact of social and economic change in ways that are unique in their direct emotional power. Often caricatured as naive and simple, Clare is in fact among the most emotively intense poets of the century.

In 1832, Clare was impoverished by the combined forces of nature (failed harvests) and society (the Acts of Enclosure and Corn Laws by which the parliamentary classes attempted to protect landed interests). Clare was ordered by the Earl of

Fitzwilliam to leave the rural tenement he had occupied since birth. His habits before this relocation show just how localized many rural lives were: the neighbouring parish seemed like a different world and parish boundaries were like borders between warring nations. Within months of his transposition to a new cottage in Northborough, Clare's worldview was disoriented, his spirit and sanity broken. This is how he recorded the experience:

> I've left my own old home of homes
> Green fields and ever pleasant place
> The summer like a stranger comes
> I pause and hardly know her face
>
> The stream it is a naked stream
> Where we on Sundays used to ramble
> The sky hangs oer a broken dream
> The brambles dwindled to a bramble.

Soon, Clare was forced to leave Northborough too, confined to an asylum from the 1830s until his death in 1864.

Clare's tragic tale was precipitated by a move from an old village to a recently constructed settlement, not even by the new space of the big city. The prose of Friedrich Engels is just as intense in its evocation of crumbling traditional orders, while providing a vision of the ultimate 'shock city' of the industrial revolution, Manchester. The young Engels had intended to devote his life to literature until his father, the owner of a Manchester factory, forced him into industry; his descriptions of British industry and its effects are now recognized as some of Victorian Britain's great literary non-fiction. In his twenties, having fallen under the spell of Thomas Carlyle, Engels was introduced to all the contradictions of Manchester life by an illiterate Irish servant girl, Mary Burns, with whom he conducted one side of his double life for two decades: he was both a wealthy international businessman and part of a stereotypical Victorian family in the dingiest hovels of England's new manufacturing heartland.

Human nature itself, Engels insisted, was as much a casualty of the new moral logic of the city as were the hills and vales of Lancashire or the Black Country. Engels described how people were physically changed by the demands of their new environment: stunted individuals with crushed limbs, curvature of the spine, knees bent inwards and ankles deformed, all because of malnourishment and overwork in the cramped conditions of Manchester mills or Macclesfield silk factories. But Engels was equally interested in the twisting and malformation of the *social* body under the strains of industrialization. His treatment of this theme could be remarkably consonant with the most conservative values of Victorian Britain (belying his reputation as a champion of gender equality). Engels quotes a long letter from a correspondent in Manchester whose friend, Joe, reported to him on the condition of the city's families:

> In a miserable, damp cellar, scarcely furnished … sat poor Jack near the fire, and what did he, think you? Why he sat and mended his wife's stockings with the bodkin; and as soon as he saw his old friend at the door-post, he tried to hide them. But Joe … had seen it, and said: 'Jack, what the devil art thou doing? Where is the missus? Why, is that thy work?' and poor Jack was ashamed, and said: 'No, I know this is not my work, but my poor missus is i' th' factory; she has to leave at half-past five and works till eight at night, and then she is so knocked up that she cannot do aught when she gets home, so I have to do everything for her what I can, for I have no work, nor had any for more nor three years, and I shall never have any more work while I live,' and then he wept a big tear.

Family was the central unit of social organization for the Victorians: the base upon which all else was built. Distinctions drawn between different familial roles – father, mother, male and female children – were intensely differentiated and deeply entrenched. Urban centres, which often took work away from the home and into large mills and factories, therefore, seemed to threaten the social order. It is a measure of just how ingrained this family ideology was that even a radical like Engels considers its subversion to be an unwarrantable aberration and threat to human dignity:

> Can anyone imagine a more insane state of things than that described in this letter? And yet this condition, which unsexes the man and takes from the woman all womanliness without being able to bestow upon the man true womanliness, or the woman true manliness – this condition which degrades, in the most shameful way, both sexes, and, through them, Humanity, is the last result of our much-praised civilisation, the final achievement of all the efforts and struggles of hundreds of generations to improve their own situation and that of their posterity.

In this way, the changing geographies of rural and urban Britain were seen as changing geographies of the human spirit. Since identity is formed in social relationships, and cities changed the nature of social interaction, what it meant to be a person – how the relationships between humanity, nature, and, in this deeply religious society, God, were understood – required new conceptualization in an unprecedented industrial landscape.

Edinburgh: the Athens (and Paris) of the North

Scotland's importance to nineteenth-century Britain must not be underestimated. It was Scotland, in the eighteenth century, that dragged British ideas into the modern world. Then (as, perhaps, now) Edinburgh was Britain's most vibrant city, boasting more leaders in the sciences, politics, literature, and philosophy than any other place. British ideals were founded upon the economics of Adam Smith and the literary romanticism of Walter Scott, as well as the political thought of individuals such as James Mill and cultural criticism of writers including Thomas Carlyle. The changing role of Edinburgh across the first half of the nineteenth century is a useful case study in integration and diversity.

In 1800, Edinburgh's cultural and intellectual links were as much with Paris as with London (this was a measure of the tensions that persisted between the four nations of the British Isles). By the beginning of the Victorian period, however, this situation was changing, and Edinburgh's intellectual vibrancy was communicated southward by major organs of cultural circulation such as the *Edinburgh Review*. The *Review*'s articles were exceptionally long, critical, and intellectually robust; ranging across the arts and sciences, literature, religion, philosophy, and current affairs, they gave combative thinkers such as Carlyle the space and freedom to develop resonant statements on the era's definitive questions. Other Edinburgh publications such as *Blackwood's Edinburgh Magazine* and *Chambers' Edinburgh Journal* carried almost equal cultural weight and self-consciously made certain that their city of origin was emblazoned in their titles. They were consumed around Britain, ensuring that readers in Manchester or Birmingham were just as likely to absorb ideas from Edinburgh as they were ideas from London.

However, Edinburgh could still seem to carry a whiff of danger. The new science of geology was developed on Scotland's west coast, and the first struggles between radical geologists who undermined literal readings of the Old Testament and conservative geologists who aimed to harmonize their theories with the Bible were fought in Edinburgh. Other new sciences were also Edinburgh innovations, and many were run through with radical, democratic potential. Phrenology, a voguish science of the early

Victorian years, claimed to assess character and ability by analysing the structure of an individual's skull. It implied the possibility of a new rational social order. If good character and intellectual ability could be measured from physiology, then status could be assigned according to anatomically quantifiable skill, rather than through the mechanisms of a hereditary aristocracy. Historians of science have shown how important phrenology was in generating a radical 'alternative view of social change and self-help'.

In keeping with the city's Enlightenment credentials, Edinburgh also maintained stronger links with European thought than most English cities did, absorbing French and German radicalism in ways that London resisted. It is no coincidence that Britain's greatest literary export of the early nineteenth century, Walter Scott, was published in Edinburgh. Nor is it surprising that the early Victorian who played the most significant role in introducing new philosophical developments in Europe to British readers was the Scot who inspired Engels, Thomas Carlyle.

Carlyle was, however, representative of a new generation of early Victorian Scottish thinkers who were less emphatically 'Scottish' than their predecessors. Where David Hume and Adam Smith had operated in networks that linked Edinburgh and Paris, Carlyle and other leading Scots of the early nineteenth century, such as James Mill, did not just communicate their ideas south via the *Edinburgh Review*, they moved to London and built emphatically British careers in the metropolis. They were icons of Britishness rather than Scottishness. Although Edinburgh's Victorian history is one of relative decline, it can also be represented as one of conquest: British culture increasingly embodied ideals that had once been associated with Edinburgh. Victorian historians, paraphrasing the Latin poet Horace, liked to talk of Athens and Rome as intertwined through two forms of conquest: the Roman empire achieved military conquest of Greece, but Greek culture enacted a more fundamental conquest of Roman consciousness. In a similar way, 'the Athens of the North' colonized the mind of the apparently more powerful imperial metropolis, London.

1837–48: a decade of rail and radicalism

At the beginning of the Victorian period, Edinburgh was still not connected to other British cities by rail. The new line, opened in 1840, was part of a railway boom that transformed Britain in the first decade of the Victorian period. This was the era of great railway engineers George Stephenson, Joseph Locke, and Isambard Kingdom Brunel. By 1848, a quarter of a million workers (known as navvies) were toiling to excavate cuttings, dig tunnels, and lay iron rails, which now stretched some 8,000 miles.

The railways boomed at a moment of intense political agitation. The new political settlement of 1832 had extended the franchise but, in making middle-class status a voting requirement, had emphatically excluded the working classes from power. Over the following two decades, the new geography formed by steam travel revolutionized the possibilities for British politics. Movements could now be national in scope and diverse in their regional make-up. The Anti-Corn Law League, for instance, was founded in Manchester by a manufacturer from Sussex (Richard Cobden), a carpet maker from Rochdale (John Bright), and a Scottish journalist (James Wilson). This agitation, in which the North West of England was as weighty a presence as the capital, was emphatically a product of the new Victorian geography.

THE RISE OF RAIL

- The 'age of steam transport' began with coal-powered locomotives as substitutes for horses on existing wagonways. Early locomotives lacked the power to transport heavy loads long distances.
- The Manchester–Liverpool railway company offered a prize to the engineer who could build a locomotive of less than six tons that could pull three times its own weight at over ten miles per hour. This was won in 1820 by the Tyneside engineer George Stephenson.

- The 'age of rail' is often said to have begun in 1825 with the opening of the Stockton to Darlington railway: it linked the collieries of County Durham to the River Tees, facilitating transport of coal to London, but the power of locomotives was still limited; part of the journey was accomplished by horse.
- The Manchester–Liverpool line opened in 1830 was the first to be operated entirely by steam.
- The success of this line led to widespread imitation. Two 'railway manias', involving enormous private expenditure, on the promise of vast profits, took place in 1836–7 and 1844–7. This was now very big business.
- In 1836, £22.9 million was committed to almost 1,000 miles of rail by 29 companies.
- The peak of the next boom occurred in 1846: £132.6 million was spent on over 4,500 miles of line by a staggering 272 railway companies.
- The capital for these projects came from diverse sources. A significant proportion was the direct product of West Indies slavery. Much was raised by shares and loans, including substantial input from the North West of England rather than London.

As the largest of these radical political movements, Chartism is revelatory in terms of the new balance between integration and diversity. Although ostensibly a single movement, which historians have used to prove the existence of a shared working-class consciousness by the 1840s, local varieties of Chartism were remarkably distinctive. United by their campaigns for the six points of the People's Charter, the cultures of Chartism in different regions were profoundly diverse. Birmingham Chartism was not straightforwardly class-focused: it had a much stronger middle-class input than the movement in, for instance, Newcastle. Manchester, the 'inky-skied' engine room of the industrial revolution, was Chartism's powerhouse: it contained, as Engels noted, the greatest suffering and oppression, and therefore the most organized political movements and the largest number of socialists, of all British cities. However, it is even more revealing that the place in which Chartism spilled over into the most expansive violence was Newport in South Wales. Here, national grievances were piled onto class antagonisms, which in turn exacerbated religious divisions: the history of English–Welsh tension was enough to give Chartist agitation the teeth that it lacked elsewhere in Britain.

It was rail, however, that made these regional Chartisms cohere into a coalition. Chartist leaders travelled Britain, spreading the ideals of democratic representation to audiences in all major industrial centres. Their publications, such as the Leeds-based *Northern Star* (1837–52), were given rapid national circulation thanks to new rail links. Indeed, the geographies of rail dictated the patterns of Chartism. The first pivotal event in Chartist campaigns came when leaders from around Britain, including the two most famous Chartists (the Welsh agitator John Frost and the Irish orator Fergus O'Connor), travelled by train to London and presented their demands to Parliament.

This period of British radicalism is often said to have ended in 1848 when Chartist leaders capitulated, accepting from Parliament a settlement that fell far short of their demand for universal manhood suffrage. But this abrupt ending does not capture what really happened. Rather than disappearing, radicalism underwent further transformations of geographical horizon. As the social historian Margot Finn has demonstrated, radicalism after 1848 was a much more transnational, Europe-wide phenomenon than it had been in the first Victorian decade. Chartism was therefore a key moment. Its regional diversities hark back to localized radicalisms of the eighteenth century; yet its phenomenal reach and use of the concept of class to unite geographically distant groups prefigures the transnational, socialist, radicalism of the twentieth.

Inventing Wales

The Welsh radicalism that exploded into view with the Chartist Newport Rising was heavily mythologized. It drew on folk and historical heroes from the biblical Rebecca to the medieval prince Owain Glyndwr and the modern rebel Dic Penderyn. The biographies of these iconic figures were embellished to generate a sense of distinctiveness and separateness in the age-old conflict between the Welsh nation and its overbearing neighbour. This captures one of the strangest features of the persistent regionality of Victorian Britain, which is often captured in a phrase popularized by the historians Eric Hobsbawm and Terence Ranger, 'The Invention of Tradition'. Across the eighteenth century, but particularly in the nineteenth, each of the four nations resisted pressures towards homogenization by producing elaborate ideas about a supposedly age-old national identity. These involved new material symbols of identity, including clothes and architecture, as well as new stories of national development and belonging. The Scottish examples of this invention are the earliest and the best known: the system of clan tartans and the kilt, for instance, were co-opted as new symbols of national character.

This nation-building exercise involved creatively rereading the past. For instance, all battles from Bannockburn to Culloden became conflicts between 'the oppressive English' and 'the heroic Scots'. This eclipsed other interpretations of those moments, including readings of Culloden as the triumph of lowland Scotland over the Highland clans, which paved the way for the Edinburgh Enlightenment and began the most glorious period in Scottish history.

Nation building meant not just the creative rewriting of history, but also full-blown forgery. As the literary scholar Nick Groom has noted, the culture of British Romanticism that inspired this nationalism 'would have been very different without literary forgery – indeed it may not have recognisably existed at all'. In England, Thomas Chatterton falsified the writings of an invented fifteenth-century monk before committing, aged seventeen, one of the most famous suicides in history. In Wales, Iolo Morganwg invented a supposedly ancient druidic tradition as the core of his new vision of Welshness. Most famously of all, Thomas MacPherson, in the 1760s, had forged a Scottish tradition of epic poetry telling the stories of mythic heroes such as Fingal and Ossian. His verse was a sensation, which duped British and European *littérateurs* for decades. The Ossian fraud became, as Thomas Curley has shown, 'a seismograph of the fragile unity within restive diversity of imperial Great Britain'.

By the Victorian period, British culture was awash with works that attempted to draw sharp distinctions between the Anglo-Saxon and the Celt. To many Metropolitan writers, such as Matthew Arnold (writing in the 1860s), even Englishness was a product of the blending of oppositional Celtic and Anglo-Saxon characteristics. The Celt was 'against the despotism of fact', ill-equipped for the hard science of government, but wonderfully imaginative and poetic: in Arnold's words 'if Celticism had not moulded England she could not have produced Shakespeare'.

To those in Scotland, Ireland, or Wales, Arnold's vision of Britain was unpalatably Anglocentric with its assumption that the English had taken the best, while rejecting the worst of Celticism. Efforts to define the Celt in stark contrast to Anglo-Saxon culture are perhaps seen most clearly in the invention of Wales. Throughout the nineteenth century, visions of Welsh distinctiveness were formalized in an increasing range of institutions and cultural practices.

The figure of the bard, a favourite of early nineteenth-century romantics, was revived as the symbol of a folkish but artistic national character, while the figure of the druid became an anti-Anglican icon, representing both Welsh closeness to nature and independence from English authority. By the mid-nineteenth century, both these figures were built into the most characteristic institution of Welsh language culture: the Eisteddfod. These competitive literary and cultural festivals were an innovation of the late eighteenth century, which only really took their modern form after 1819. Yet they were self-conscious throwbacks to a golden era of medieval Welsh culture. Many of the early prizes, awarded for competitions in poetry and story-telling, as the historian of Wales, Prys Morgan, notes, were awarded to works on historical themes, including:

> Wales from Cadwaladr the Blessed to Llywelyn the Last, Edward I's massacre of the Welsh Bards in 1282, and so on, which had a profound effect in creating interest in Welsh traditions (sometimes quite bogus ones) amongst the people.

It was in the Eisteddfodau of the post-Napoleonic era that the idea of Welsh bards as direct heirs to the ancient druidic tradition was invented, as the rites and rituals, mythology, religion, and character of modern Wales were explained through this ancient pedigree.

The driving force of this new vision of Welshness, Iolo Morganwg, had set up small bardic groups across Wales in the 1800s. In 1819, these groups, known as the Gorseddau of Bards, were grafted onto the young Eisteddfod tradition, granting these festivals a mythology that made them far more than literary competitions. To this day, Eisteddfodau are still overseen by a committee of artistic druids.

These 'invented traditions' emphasized a Celtic history, mythology, music, and language that were emphatically separate from those of England. It is no coincidence that the nineteenth century, when economic and political pressures generated new connections across the British Isles, was the key period in the creation of a vibrant new Welsh culture that suggested Wales to be a coherent, self-contained cultural entity.

This culture did not go unopposed. The Welsh language had long faced English hostility (the later middle ages, for instance, had seen Welsh-language bards outlawed), and the nineteenth-century resurgence of Welsh national identity faced similar repression.

In 1846, Parliament commissioned a report on the role of the Welsh language in education. This was a direct response to Welsh political agitations and was intended to ascertain why Wales was 'prone to lawlessness'. The three Anglican barristers who compiled the report (published in 1847) were deeply disparaging about the morality and capabilities of the Welsh. They saw the Welsh language as the principal barrier to progress; yet even they voiced concern at the arbitrary humiliation sometimes meted out to children caught speaking Welsh in schools. The Welsh language was put under great pressure in the second half of the century, with the emergence of an establishment consensus that economic growth was predicated on a homogeneous British polity. This pitted an economic and political vision of modernity, which favoured integration, against a social and cultural modernity, which favoured strong national identities and new adaptations of deep-rooted traditions. Welsh culture embodies, in extreme form, tensions that existed throughout the British Isles.

This chapter has hinted at several themes that will be significant throughout the book. The first is that geography mattered. Changes in the demographic make-up of the British Isles had a substantial impact on everything from the possibilities of radical politics to the provision of religious or, later, educational needs. The numbers involved here are less significant than the psychological and social impact of such transformative developments. The second implication is that all the people of Britain held multiple identities in fragile balance. Local, regional, and national identities interacted with identities of class, gender, and ethnicity, of urban or rural interest groups and religious denominations, to produce complex forms of differentiation and belonging. To be a Victorian was no more a straightforward form of identity than to be an inhabitant of a twenty-first-century nation state.

4

Knowing the world: the inventions of empire

An insular history of Britain (and there have been too many such) is quite inadequate … Britain developed as an essential part of a global economy, and more particularly as the centre of that vast formal or informal 'empire' on which its fortunes so largely rested. To write about this country without also saying something about the West Indies and India, about Argentina and Australia, is unreal.

Eric Hobsbawm, *Industry & Empire* (1968)

The term Victorian suggests strict geographical limits. It denotes a period in the history of Britain and, perhaps, the British Empire or (in the most expansive usages) the English-speaking world. Yet the Victorians were a global people. To adopt the attitude of a 2013 textbook of Victorian history that admitted that it would avoid topics such as 'empire and foreign policy' is to give up any hope of understanding the Victorians.

By virtue of new or intensified varieties of global interaction, the things Victorians wore, ate, and drank, the books and newspapers they read, the shows and exhibitions they saw were all marked by interactions with a wider world. This engagement took many forms, ranging from outright military conflict, to commitment to international Free Trade, scholarly study of customs or religious traditions, and the consumption of global goods and ideas. Internationalism was also written into national identities: many Victorians saw themselves as outward-looking actors on a world stage. The lives of explorers, pioneers, missionaries, and seafarers were given glamour in poetry, fiction, art, and song, as well as reams of travel narrative and biography.

Victorian infrastructure and institutions were built on the imperial expansion of previous decades. Even after the abolition of slavery in the British Empire (1833), an extraordinary proportion of industry was funded by the proceeds of the trade because, when abolition was enforced, slave-owners had received financial compensation for loss of slaves. Much of this money (over £20 million in total) was invested in Britain, founding new firms and permitting the expansion of others. An extraordinary number of Victorian banks, docks, and railways were built upon this slave compensation.

This global interaction is easy to oversimplify. London was not an all-controlling hub with its global empire as a vast 'periphery'; nor was metropolitan culture simply moulded by outside influences that flooded inexorably in. Ideas, materials, and people flowed between regions, nations, and continents, not in single lines but in complex matrices of influence and exchange. Knowledge of the world was never made by lone explorers but in relationships between cultures; it was shaped by negotiators, translators, messengers, merchants, and spies, who created productive fusions of diverse traditions such as Hindu astronomy and Newtonian mechanics.

The administration of the British Empire can illustrate some of these complexities. When, in 1882, Britain occupied Egypt, a host of British politicians and administration were shipped to Cairo. Yet few came from Britain: many were sent from posts in the Indian civil service. They were British, upper class, and white with more knowledge of ancient Greek and Latin than of Indian languages; some had undertaken brief schooling in Britain, but some of the most powerful, including the engineer responsible for transforming Egyptian agriculture, William Willcocks, had never even set foot in the British Isles. Other leading figures in the early years of British power in Egypt had made their names serving outside the empire, in China, Palestine, or Brazil. One such example, General Charles George Gordon, became a national hero when he died mounting a foolhardy escapade in the Egyptian Sudan. He had created his extraordinary reputation as an adventurer in China and as a pious, eccentric, seeker after Anglican origins in Jerusalem.

Individuals such as Willcocks and Gordon embodied all the values and characteristics of Victorianism. Yet Britain was not their 'centre' with the rest of the empire a periphery. For Willcocks, India was home and the terrain that defined his perspective on the world. Jerusalem was the clear centre of Gordon's religious worldview. In 1958, the poet and critic T.S. Eliot looked back on the life of Rudyard Kipling, an eminent Victorian, for whom India was far more 'home' than Britain was: 'he had been a citizen of the British Empire long before he naturalised himself … in … England'. There were thousands of other individuals about whom this could have been written.

Although Victorian interaction with the world cannot be reduced to imperialism, empire is the single biggest fact to be dealt with in this chapter. Imperialism coloured a great deal of Britain's interaction with other parts of the globe, just as empire formed many British people's vision of their place in the world order. It provided vocations in colonial administration for the well-to-do, and work in infrastructure and construction for the less well-off. At its peak, early in the twentieth century, there were 125 subjects of the empire for every individual in Britain.

Yet, paradoxically, incidents around the empire did not always arouse a great deal of interest in Britain. Major events such as the transition to self-governance of what is now Canada, or the catastrophic defeat of British troops in Afghanistan in 1844, sometimes occurred without attracting substantial public attention. A Victorian quip, popular in the 1860s, even suggested that the quickest way to clear the House of Commons was to start a debate on the governance of India.

These paradoxes cannot easily be smoothed over. One of the fiercest of all scholarly disagreements about the Victorians concerns the extent to which British culture was 'imperial' in nature. In one of the classic studies of imperial history, *At Home with the Empire*, Catherine Hall and Sonya Rose show just how great was the prevalence of imperial things and imperial ideas in British culture. Other historians, such as John Mackenzie, have explored the multitude of ways in which empire shaped culture. Some students at my university recently put together a superb research project tracing the imperial origins of the ingredients of a Victorian Christmas pudding: with rum and sugar from the West Indies, Australian currants, South African raisins, English cooking apples, and Scottish beef suet, a single pudding could be a truly transnational product.

However, the historian of empire Bernard Porter argues that, although Britain was awash with imperial things, 'dissemination' is not the same as 'reception': it was quite possible for British people, surrounded by the products of empire, to go about their daily lives with very little awareness of the origins or meaning of what they saw and used. Although many historians have tried (and failed) to reconcile the view of an imperial culture put forward by Hall and Rose with that of imperial ignorance set out by Porter, these two perspectives are opposed: they cannot both be right. It is probably the case that more historians now favour Hall and Rose's views, but there are still leading historians who adopt the alternative position, and it seems unlikely that this debate will ever be resolved. If it is, cultural developments in the present, rather than matters of historical fact, will be what change people's minds.

This chapter will provide a basic outline of a history of the British Empire in the Victorian period. However, recounting the events of empire would not go far towards showing how the movement of Victorians around the world – inside and outside empire – shaped Victorian society. In pursuing the wider goal of demonstrating the profoundly international nature of Victorian culture, this chapter will focus on one particular theme: it will be about knowledge. This will mean exploring how global travel and imperial politics were entangled with the making of scientific knowledge. Scientific exploration, colonial reconnaissance, and colonial administration were always inseparable projects. Victorian cartography, geology, evolutionary biology, and astronomy were all made on the edges of empire as much as in the scientific sanctuaries of the imperial metropolis. How did what the Victorians knew shape how and where they travelled? How did where they travelled shape what they knew?

Imperial chronology

The history of the British Empire in the nineteenth century has conventionally been divided into three periods. The first division, lasting until around 1850, includes substantial expansion. The decade after the acquisition of Western Australia (1829) saw the Falklands, South Australia, and Aden brought into the empire; New Zealand, Natal, Sind, and North Borneo were all part of 1840s expansion. This was a period when British writers showed significant interest in empire but, as Boyd Hilton has argued, this was usually 'cerebral rather than visceral'. Early Victorian writers asked what the empire could do for Britain. However, they were usually thinking in terms of population and commerce; they rarely spoke of 'imperial destiny' or voiced intense ideological fervour.

This was also the period when emigration became a national fascination. As the historian of empire Andrew Thompson has shown, music hall songs in the 1840s were full of tales of emigrant experience. The National Colonization Society (1830) and

Colonial Land and Emigration Commission (1840) assisted the movement of British people to settler colonies such as Australia and New Zealand. These were substantial, powerful organizations such that Jeffrey Richards has called the latter 'one of the most important agencies of government planning in the Victorian age'.

The mid-Victorian period, from the 1850s to the 1870s, has traditionally been seen as a time when engagement in empire waned: expansion slowed, public interest declined, and there were halting moves towards self-governance in the colonies (renamed dominions) that British people had settled. This included British North America, which was soon rechristened Canada.

The final decades of the century are characterized, undoubtedly correctly, as the most raucously imperialistic. They are inflected with jingoism, culminating in the 'khaki fever' of the second Boer War. This enthusiasm for acquisition was galvanized by conviction that Europeans ruled the world by right of race and divine blessing. This is, however, also a period when vocal opposition to empire emerged: opinion was not just becoming more imperialistic, it was polarizing rapidly.

JINGOISM

British high imperialism after 1870 was characterized by extravagant self-belief and conviction that the British Empire ruled for the good of the world. The idea of the 'white man's burden' implied that innate superiority gave the British not just the right but the responsibility to govern other peoples. 'We are called upon to rule,' wrote Anthony Trollope in 1872, 'not for our glory but for their happiness.' The strongest statements of this proud nationalism tended to be defensive: they were made whenever cracks appeared in the veneer of Britain's apparent invincibility. They were also a response to increasingly vocal liberal critics of imperialism.

Late Victorian popular culture was full of imperial and militaristic themes. In 1878, a music hall song performed by G.H. Macdermott (known simply as Macdermott's War Song) expressed British hostility to Russian power: 'We don't want to fight but by jingo if we do/We've got the ships, we've got the men, we've got the money too'. Responding to this song, the radical politician George Holyoake coined the term 'jingoism'. This was soon a well-known word, used to denote aggressive patriotism, advocacy of the use of force in foreign affairs, and parochial conviction that Britain was superior to every other nation of the world.

As always with such neat typologies, this traditional view has great illustrative value but is only accurate at the most superficial level. It is very easy, for instance, to find a host of statements of imperial destiny and British superiority from the early Victorian period. This is especially true if we turn to places other than the region most frequently used as a measure of imperial ideas, India. In the 1840s, for instance, views of the Arab world and Ottoman Empire were inflected with uniquely intense Islamophobia. Leading figures in British culture, such as curators at the British Museum, regularly voiced the 'right' of a Christian people to rule over 'benighted' Muslims. Similarly, one of the most intense moments of jingoistic fervour and British immersion in questions of imperial power came not in the 1890s but in the aftermath of the Indian Uprising of 1857.

The world in maps: making British India

Maps matter. They do not simply reflect the world as it is, but shape the way people imagine the spaces in which they live, work, or travel. Among the most vivid explanations of this is a plotline in the television show *The West Wing*. In this scene, an organization called Cartographers for Social Justice presents to the Presidential office a campaign to change the world maps used in American schools. The offending maps use the same convention for converting the three-dimensional globe into a two-dimensional picture that the Victorians used (and which is still by far the most familiar in America and Europe). This convention is known as the Mercator projection. As the Cartographers for Social Justice point out, the Mercator projection exaggerates the scale of Europe and North America, marginalizing vast continents such as Africa and South America. On the world maps we share with the Victorians, Greenland appears to be a similar size to Africa. Africa is in fact fourteen times bigger. In pressing for the more representative Peters projection as a replacement for Mercator, the cartographers hope to challenge North Americans' vision of themselves at the centre of the world order.

Few Victorians, including those who set off to explore, conquer, or convert parts of Africa or Asia, had any real conception of the smallness and marginality of their islands. Even the relatively recent convention of placing North at the top of maps had conspired to make Europe seem like the centre of the world. Victorian homes and school rooms contained supposedly authoritative images, which made Britain seem large, geographically central, and globally significant. The famous crimson ink used to mark domains subject to British imperial rule gave Victorians a vision of British economic and political power radiating from the map's centre to its edges. Spreading to the same extent as this ink, they assumed, were commerce, law, and order, as well as Christianity and a favourite Victorian abstraction, 'civilization'.

Not just world maps, but also maps of much smaller regions reinforced particular cultural messages. There were soon hundreds of atlases available, charting modern populations or the civilizations of the ancient world, the geography of world religions, or the expanding spheres of missionary activity. While the Ordnance Survey plotted the coasts and contours of Britain, other cartographers eased the passage of British power by charting diverse regions of the globe. Their first priorities had often been to map tides and prevailing winds in order that naval and cargo ships might ply global waters swiftly and safely. Inland, the East India Company gathered knowledge of terrain and human geography as a precondition of each step in its expansion. The surveys they conducted contained information on people, politics, resources, and culture, as well as the geographical data reproduced in the visual maps that graced the walls of their council chambers. The local sources they initially drew on, such as pre-British Mughal land records, make certain that any distinction between 'European science' and other forms of knowledge is impossible to draw. Indeed, a recent multi-authored book, *The Brokered World: Go-Betweens and Global Intelligence*, has shown just how much the ways in which Europeans saw the world was not new or path-breaking but was derived from the sophisticated and wide-ranging knowledge of local guides and intermediaries.

THE EAST INDIA COMPANY

The 'Governor and Company of Merchants of London Trading Into the East Indies' received its royal charter from Elizabeth I in 1600. It was later renamed the 'Honourable East India Company'. This was a 'joint stock' venture, with aristocrats and merchants owning its shares: the state did not possess shares or operate direct control. The organization pursued trade on the Indian subcontinent and in China. This commerce was initially in spices but later in opium, saltpetre, and other commodities. Its members became wealthy and powerful, establishing huge estates in Britain and a powerful lobby in Parliament.

In the 1750s, European competition over trade in India led to the Seven Years' War during which the East India Company, under Robert Clive, defeated French interests to gain military and political supremacy in Bengal. By the early nineteenth century, Company control extended across much of the subcontinent. However, the British government was uneasy about the Company's power and a series of parliamentary acts from 1773 to 1833 gradually limited its independence. In the aftermath of the 1857 Indian Uprising, during which agents of the East India Company committed numerous atrocities, the British government nationalized the Company, and in 1874 it was dissolved completely.

Cartographers arrived in India in search of both scientific knowledge and monetary fortune. Their maps of supposedly 'unclaimed' parts of the Indian subcontinent gave British administrators a sense of advantage over other European powers and even of entitlement to rule the spaces they recorded. It was at precisely the beginning of the Victorian period that the Surveyor General in India, George Everest (after whom the world's tallest mountain is named), changed the practices of cartographers, attempting to undermine reliance on local knowledge by importing precision instruments from Europe. The expensive new trigonometric surveys of the 1830s and 1840s were conducted with mathematical techniques involving calculus and Newtonian mechanics, which Everest believed Indian people were not capable of using. The historian of science Matthew Edney has demonstrated just how little difference these changes of technique and technology made to the quality or precision of mapping: this was not a scientific 'leap forward' so much as a change of ideology.

Technology, the practice of mapping, and the ideology of British India all developed in a complex web of interactions (one was not the single cause of the others). An illustration of this can be found in the observation towers that Everest built across the populated plains of India. These met with concerted local opposition, especially when their sightlines were cleared of highly valued trees. Enforcing this scientific architecture was an act of pacification and control as well as scientific discovery: it was an attempt to change the situation whereby, as the politician G.O. Trevelyan vividly wrote, imperial civilization extended 'one hundred yards on either side of the railway track'.

What Everest and his peers were undertaking was an attempt to transform an enormous, diverse, and ambiguous geographical space into a single, knowable, and bounded subject called India: they were creating the idea of India itself. In the words of Edney, '*British* India, which was otherwise a quite arbitrary entity, was naturalized by the British to be a constant, timeless, "natural", uniform geographical entity, political state, and cultural nation'. Given that India is more a continent than a country, with a diverse population speaking nearly a thousand languages and congregated in hundreds of ethnic and caste communities, establishing this coherence was far from easy. There were, in fact, never more than 100,000 British people amidst an Indian population numbering nearly 300 million.

The 'cartographic ideal' of a systematic and totalized image of India was, in practice, as Edney puts it, 'cartographic anarchy', as too much information of too diverse a kind flowed into the East India Company's offices. The single image of India that was created was a compromise, but it contributed to a 'cartographic culture' in which unity was asserted through careful selection of the information contained in the maps consulted by everyone from generals and administrators to schoolchildren. Edney's claim is dramatic but justified: 'the empire might have defined the map's extent, but mapping defined the empire's nature'.

The fruits of not knowing: imperial crises from Afghanistan to Jamaica

The British Empire was founded on a combination of direct force, ideological persuasion, and the acquisition of knowledge. When the empire faced crises, it was often because this knowledge had failed: the British had misunderstood the worlds into which they were intruding. The most potent early Victorian example of this is the First Afghan War.

In 1840, India was 'the jewel in the crown' of empire: a vast source of material resources and money. Indeed, as the British government worked to reduce the independence of the East India Company, it was slowly transformed from an unrestrained adventuring organization into an enormous tax-collecting machine. India was also a major field for British economic expansion.

Many of the elite of Victorian Britain distrusted manufacture and refused to 'dirty their hands' in industry: the alternatives they chose were commercial ventures on the Indian subcontinent, including large-scale import and export. In a profoundly influential book, P.J. Cain and A.G. Hopkins termed this international phenomenon *Gentlemanly Capitalism*.

In the light of the economic importance of India, the British were neurotic about security. In particular, they feared a Russian challenge to their dominance on the subcontinent. In order to increase their claim on resources, military leaders in India had greatly exaggerated this threat. British policy makers looked to Afghanistan as a buffer zone between India and Russian interests. The disastrous results provide an early illustration of what could happen when ambitions stretched beyond geographical and social knowledge.

In 1840, the Governor General of India, Lord Auckland, speculated – nervously – that the Emir of Afghanistan, Dost Mohammad, might be pro-Russian. He decided to install an exiled, British-friendly Afghan, Shah Shuja, in his place. Auckland ordered an invasion of Kabul, using Hindu troops from British India. This momentarily seemed successful, but its later fate earned it the enduring name of 'Auckland's Folly'. Conquest was followed by hasty, piecemeal attempts to 'Anglicize' Afghanistan, which demonstrated total ignorance of the tribal structure of the region. By November 1841, riots had broken out and the British consul had been hacked to death. *Social* knowledge had failed.

The next error was a retreat of the entire British garrison towards Jalalabad. Here, *geographical* knowledge failed. Stranded amidst mountain passes in unforeseen sub-zero temperatures, with soldiers suffering from frostbite, the troops were set upon by the Dost's supporters. Armed with little more than knives, these Afghans defeated a British army of 15,000 so conclusively that only one individual – a medical officer – made it through to Jalalabad.

Since power, like beauty, is in part in the eye of the beholder, the British were desperate to redress this humiliation. Their answer was a brutal, vengeful assault on Kabul, which included such unnecessary acts as blowing up the city's famous bazaar and incinerating nearby villages. Having abandoned the aspiration to make use of Afghanistan, the troops left as quickly as they arrived. Unsurprisingly, Dost Mohammad now governed a large population that was fiercely anti-British.

The consequences of this debacle stretched far beyond Afghanistan, and they were cultural as much as military. The political class, it was argued, had failed the soldiery, and authority was shifted towards the military. But the most profound consequence of these events was a shift in worldview. Ironically (given that the wanton aggression in these events was largely British), the racialized descriptions of Afghan tribesmen, characterized by 'savagery', 'treachery', and 'bloodthirsty butchery', contributed to an intensified feeling that a huge and unbridgeable gap existed between 'civilized Europeans' and non-European 'savages'.

Ideology in British India at the beginning of the century had held that all peoples were essentially the same; they were just at different stages of one process of development. But the new ideology suggested that some races were not capable of development at all. This view did not yet suffuse culture in Britain, but as the Victorian period went on, and particularly after the 1870s, the British interpreted the world in these racialized terms.

The First Afghan War was a turning point in other ways too. Imperial prestige was irredeemably damaged. This encouraged Indian opposition to the British and the stage was set for conflicts such as the Indian Uprising of 1857. Far more widely reported in Britain than the First Afghan War, the events of 1857 were conceptualized within the same framework. The British were presented as civilized and irreproachable: the massacres they carried out were widely ignored. In contrast, 'rebellious' Indians were portrayed as utterly wanton in their depravity. Rumours of the rape of white women by Indian men were widespread (although there is no evidence that any women stationed in

India reported such events having occurred). Here was further evidence of a supposed gulf between races.

Over the following decades, debates about racial hierarchies and human difference were triggered by other imperial crises. Among the most famous of these was the Morant Bay massacre. This occurred in 1865 when, after protests against British rule in Jamaica, Governor John Eyre dispatched British troops who savagely and indiscriminately butchered 439 Jamaicans, arresting 354 more who were subsequently executed. As one British soldier put it, 'we slaughtered all before us … man or woman or child'.

Where events in Kabul and the Afghan mountains had been largely ignored in Britain, this atrocity caused a public outcry. Many of the most eminent Victorians published for and against Eyre. Perhaps surprisingly, many of the great literary moralizers and churchmen, including Charles Dickens, John Ruskin, Charles Kingsley, and Thomas Carlyle, chose to justify Eyre's actions in terms of the lesser humanity of the people of Jamaica. Carlyle's 1849 'Occasional Discourse on the Negro Question' was revised and republished for the occasion: it shows just how authoritarian and reactionary this thinker had become in the decades since his great humanistic works of the early 1830s. It was, however, an indicator of increasingly intolerant social attitudes, as well as one man's ungraceful ageing.

In contrast, many of Eyre's fiercest critics, and defenders of the dignity of Jamaican people, were men of science. These included Charles Darwin, T.H. Huxley (the palaeontologist known as 'Darwin's Bulldog'), and the philosopher and popularizer of science Herbert Spencer (now vilified for his views on race). This is worth remembering, because 'social Darwinism' and evolutionary biology are often considered to be root causes of late Victorian racism. They were certainly not causes, although they were two among very many sources of apparent authority, ranging from eugenics to scripture, that could be used to justify and conceptualize racism.

Imperial species: Charles Darwin and the *Beagle* voyage

It is no surprise to see Darwin's name on a list of commentators on empire. Indeed, Darwin is a prominent example of the inextricable bonds between empire and science. The combined advancement of scientific and imperial interests has a long history. Explorers such as James Cook and entrepreneurs such as the mercantile geologist Roderick Murchison had made science into a function of empire, but also assured that empire facilitated science. By the Victorian period, it may appear that much of the most important imperial science followed the flag rather than actively advancing it, but this did not reduce the strength of the bond between knowledge and power.

Darwin, like several other Victorian biologists, began his career in the real-life laboratories of ocean and island that comprised the imperial colonies most distant from Europe. Almost by accident, the young Darwin had become a ship's naturalist destined for the desolate coasts of Patagonia. Planning to write a book on geology, he soon came to see this region as an extraordinary resource: a place close to the conditions of the early world. An earthquake, in particular, produced a visceral response:

> A bad earthquake at once destroys our oldest associations: the earth, the very emblem of solidity, has moved beneath our feet like a thin crust over fluid – one second of time has created in the mind a strange idea of insecurity, which hours of reflection would not have produced.

Darwin also began to notice multitudes of fossilized creatures. Some were small, such as the brachiopods he found in rocks on the Falklands. Others were more dramatic, such as the giant armadillo now displayed in London's Natural History Museum.

By the time they reached the Galapagos Islands, Darwin was both bewildered and fascinated by the alien creatures among which the ship's crew found themselves. Some of these, such as the giant tortoises Darwin insisted on riding, were entirely foreign. Others were strangely familiar, including the many species of finches, which had each adapted to the landscapes they lived in.

Darwin's interest slowly shifted from rocks to living things: almost all his lifelong fascinations were established on this voyage. The vast array of specimens he collected, and drawings he made, provided the raw material from which canonical texts such as *On the Origin of Species* (1859) and *The Descent of Man* (1871) were constructed. Evolution had been a widely circulated idea long before Darwin, but in the concept of natural selection (soon vulgarized as 'the survival of the fittest') he found an explanation, for how new species came into being, which had the potential to be developed into a scientific theory. It is no coincidence that Darwin's peer and rival in the development of this theory, Alfred Russell Wallace, had also been inspired by his travels around the empire's Pacific colonies.

Over the following decades, Darwin and his idea became icons of the professionalization of science. In the hands of its many publicizers, natural selection came to be far more than an individual theory. It became the epitome of a scientific principle pursued on its own terms, rather than in the service of theology. Darwin's supporters championed the professionalization of science, by which they meant both the establishment of the scientist as an independent authority, and the consolidation of the sciences as independent, centrally funded, bodies of knowledge. Darwin's blend of establishment credentials (he had attended Christ's College, Cambridge), sustained research (during his five years in 'the colonial laboratory'), and ambitious theories made him the poster boy for this new form of knowledge. The twenty-two-year-old Darwin may have almost sleepwalked into his imperial adventure, but the empire's impact on Victorian science was as great as its initial impact on Darwin himself had been.

CHARLES DARWIN: VICTORIAN NATURALIST

- Born in 1809 in Shrewsbury, Darwin was part of a prominent Victorian clan, the Darwin-Wedgwoods, which contained several members of Parliament, pioneers in the sciences, artists, poets, and industrialists.
- From 1825, Darwin attended the University of Edinburgh Medical School but with little enthusiasm. In 1828, he relocated to Christ's College, Cambridge, his father intending for him to become an Anglican clergyman.
- Darwin's 1838 publication of his journals written on the *Beagle* voyage made him a household name. His observations also aroused the interest of leading thinkers including the geologist Charles Lyell. Darwin married his cousin Emma Wedgwood in the same year.
- Between 1838 and 1859, Darwin honed his ideas on the development of species, influenced by a host of thinkers who had published on evolution over the previous century. In *On the Origin of Species* (1859), he explained how natural selection could lead to the transmutation of characteristics. This was much less controversial than most evolutionary texts of the period, as Darwin was both from a respectable social background and very careful not to make polemical claims in relation to biblical religion.
- In 1871, Darwin published a more controversial text, *The Descent of Man*. This was his first text to use the term 'evolution' and his first to extend natural selection (alongside the related idea of sexual selection) to human beings.
- Darwin died in 1882. He had expected to be buried in his local churchyard but instead was honoured by the Church of England with a lavish funeral and burial in Westminster Abbey.

Imperial observations: solar eclipse expeditions

The scientific expeditions of the Victorian period carry their fair share of gruesome and grisly endings: they make compelling stories, but not of the kind that Hollywood could endow with happy endings. Members of the Franklin Expedition, which sought the Northwest passage between the Atlantic and the Pacific, took painstaking precautions to prepare themselves and their ships, the *Erebus* and the *Terror*, to handle frozen seas. Becoming trapped in ice in 1846 did not annihilate the crew; but two years later, exposure, starvation, scurvy, and – ultimately – cannibalism did. Scientific expeditions to Africa routinely lost all or most of their members, usually to disease but sometimes to violence or shipwreck. Even as late as 1856–9, the explorers in the Burton–Speke expedition spent most of their time incapacitated by fever or under assault from the people whose territory they attempted to cross. The two leaders were phenomenally lucky to survive their quest to locate the source of the Nile; the mission itself, however, failed.

Slowly, the risks were mitigated. By the 1860s, new kinds of expedition were possible. New technologies of travel such as the steamship and rail reduced both the duration and trepidation of journeys. New medicines, including quinine, reduced susceptibility to diseases such as malaria. For expeditions in India, the telegraph permitted rapid communication of any political or medical crises that might disrupt life for both residents and travellers. All this dramatically increased the possibilities for imperial science. Not just biology and geology, but also physics and chemistry were transformed.

Astrophysics and solar physics are good examples of these developments. They were innovations of the mid-Victorian period, which gained an expansive imperial dimension in the 1860s. In particular, these sciences made solar eclipses into events of such intellectual importance that physicists and astronomers would travel thousands of miles to observe them. They went throughout the British colonies and beyond: between 1860 and 1914, around two dozen large-scale solar eclipse expeditions were conducted from Britain, taking observers to central India, Chile, Sumatra, and elsewhere.

These expeditions allow us to look at a very important aspect of both Victorian science and Victorian imperialism. This is an area that historians of science have become increasingly interested in: the practice – rather than just the ideas – of scientists. We learn as much, if not more, from asking what scientists actually did, how they made their knowledge in interaction with others and with the natural world, as we learn from asking what ideas they eventually published. Studying their practice allows us to see scientists planning the social dimension of their work, tying it to political and economic interests, and ultimately generating its moral respectability and intellectual authority.

The historian of science Alex Soojung-Kim Pang has shown just how extraordinary eclipse expeditions were. They required years of planning, which drew in scientific societies, instrument makers, chemical companies, photographic suppliers, politicians, army officers, administrators, transport officials, and many others. These plans culminated in vast voyages carrying tons of large and extremely delicate scientific instruments: glass plates could shatter, some spectroscopes were so temperature sensitive that heat from a human body could render them useless. All this effort was committed to observations lasting less than seven minutes, which could be entirely sabotaged by bad weather, famine, disease, political unrest, or mere incompetence.

Eclipses were the best guides to the nature of the sun and therefore to the physical nature of stars in general. Astronomers suspected that solar behaviour might have significant but complex meteorological effects on earth. They also aspired to understand the laws of lunar, solar, and planetary motion. However, more was at stake than this. The Royal Astronomical Society and the Royal Society used these expeditions as markers of imperial prestige: they were entangled with Britain's political and military activities. In Pang's words, linking expeditions 'rhetorically to national pride and international scientific preeminence', travellers drew favours from the Royal Navy and colonial governments. They relied on maps from organizations such as the East India Company to identify the towns and villages that would lie under the paths of eclipses. The task of collecting information about the areas that would become 'the field' drew on all the resources of the imperial state and in return glorified the imperial project as the embodiment of the scientific spirit.

In return for their valorization of empire, travelling gentlemen of science were treated as dignitaries and accorded a higher-class status when abroad than they occupied at home. The camps they occupied were calculated to communicate colonial power. Tents were borrowed from the army or civil service; they were furnished, carpeted, and equipped with guards, servants, libraries, bunting, and flags. In these imposing surroundings, astronomers would rehearse their local assistants for days before the eclipse itself.

Once under way, astronomers wrote prodigiously. They took full advantage of the new literary markets of Victorian Britain. Not just reports for scientific journals, but also travel books, guides to observation, newspaper articles, pieces for the up-market reviews and for low-market magazines poured from their pens in order to cement their reputations as authoritative witnesses and trustworthy guides to a new realm of knowledge. They did not report just what they saw in the skies, but also what they experienced on the ground and how they handled the obstacles placed in their way.

Many eclipse observers were household names and bestselling authors. Their accounts of the moment of eclipse were heavily romanticized, making full use of the 'poetics' of science: 'the decisive moment approached nearer and nearer', wrote one astrophysicist, 'with anxious care we contemplated the clouded sky, when suddenly, to our great joy, the clouds parted, and we beheld the sun, already partially eclipsed'. Observers described not just measurements but also emotions when the solar corona became visible: 'No feeling of terrified awe came over us, but a grander emotion was experienced, that of superlative sublimity'.

These ennobled feelings were often contrasted with disdain for the supposed responses of 'natives' who 'in Africa ran in great distress … [for] they could not comprehend the nature of meaning of an eclipse' or Chinese observers who 'beat their gongs all through totality' to drive away dragons. Even the most austere scientific journals published articles recounting local eclipse superstitions. Contrasts of 'Western rationality', including mastery over self and nature, with 'native superstition' are found throughout such descriptions. Superstition in late Victorian thinking was closely linked to fanaticism, and the observation of superstitious customs justified the drawing of lines of defence.

These conventions found their way around Victorian culture, including its fiction. In one of the most memorable scenes of H. Rider Haggard's *King Solomon's Mines* (1886), the British protagonists are condemned to execution by a central African tribe. By correctly predicting, and appearing to control, an eclipse, the British heroes convince the tribesmen that they have the power of gods: the result is that they rule over, rather than being victims of, the superstitious natives. As one astronomer and clergyman put it in 1871: without astronomy's aid, 'the mighty empires now consolidating … would not exist … and the hope of ultimately linking mankind into one brotherhood of God's children would be abortive'.

The world on the Victorian streets

Just as hundreds of thousands of British people emigrated abroad, hundreds of thousands of people arrived via British ports. Many of them did a great deal to shape the life of British cities. Britain's immigration laws were an invention of 1905: during the whole Victorian period Britain took in all comers. Those who arrived ranged from religious and political refugees, poor labourers and artisans, service workers, businessmen, professionals, and aristocrats, to scholars, students, writers, and artists. After the French Revolution in 1789, many French emigres made their homes in London; after the revolutions of 1848, tens of thousands of Germans did too, most notably Karl Marx and Friedrich Engels. In the 1880s, large numbers of Jews arrived as refugees from Russia, and in port cities East Indian lascars and seamen mixed with a small permanent population of Chinese traders (the first of Merseyside's Chinese laundries was opened in 1887). Students and scholars arrived from India to be taught in British universities. By 1900, it was possible to learn Hindustani, Bengali, Gujarati, or Hindu law from different Indian professors at the University of London. There were also smaller numbers of black immigrants from Africa, the West Indies, and America, many of whom fulfilled significant roles in British life. One of the most striking instances is a celebrated actor of the period, Ira Aldridge, an African American who played many of the great Shakespearean roles on major London stages, sometimes wearing white make-up. One of Britain's leading composers at the end of the century was Samuel Coleridge-Taylor, known as 'the African Mahler', whose father, a leading London physician, was from Sierra Leone. Books have been devoted to the experience and representation of these communities, ranging from Ron Greaves' *Islam in Victorian Britain* to two books entitled *Black Victorians*, one by Jan Marsh and the other by Gretchen Gerzina.

This is not to say that Britain was a happily multicultural space. British people outside major cities would have seen little of this diversity, while those within cosmopolitan urban areas were often uncomfortable with it. Many immigrant communities were ghettoized and treated with suspicion by their neighbours. As the historian Rosemary Ashton has noted, 'England opened its doors to all comers, but extended a warm embrace to no one'. All these communities were, however, observed and written about. Their appearances in urban literature remind us that the streets of British cities, just as much as the mission field or the imperial frontier, could be treated as a 'living panorama' or 'human museum' in which Victorians attempted to classify and delineate a complex global order.

It is therefore entirely unsurprising that this was the period when the desire to comprehend and order human diversity was gradually consolidated in the anthropological sciences. For much of the century, the emerging sciences of human difference maintained roots in scripture, particularly the description of the dispersion of peoples around the world in Genesis chapter 10. One major debate for early Victorians focused on the question of whether all humans originated from a single source (monogenesis) or many (polygenesis). This had profound implications for issues such as slavery. One familiar argument ran that, if Africans belonged to a different family of mankind from those who began with Adam and Eve, then they could be presented as outside the covenant between God and humanity: they need not be accorded the privileges of full human freedom; if, however, humans all originated from a single source, then slavery was un-Christian and unforgivable.

By the end of the century, the primary justifications for racism drew on the language of science more than scripture. The discovery of prehistoric humans, argued over through what became known as 'the antiquity of man' debate in the 1870s, had transformed the field. Race was widely seen to be a biological fact, defined by 'blood' and wildly divergent capabilities and character (Colin Kidd, in *The Forging of Races*, offers a wonderful dissection of this once-convincing racial science). Some argued that races of humanity were so different that interracial reproduction would result in infertile offspring. However, the anthropological sciences remained divided on all these issues. Where there were always some, such as the infamous Robert Knox (now often used by historians as exemplary of the new scientific racism), who pressed starkly racialized arguments, there were many others whose anthropological agendas stood in direct opposition to this.

ETHNOLOGY AND ANTHROPOLOGY

The term 'ethnology' was coined at the beginning of the Victorian period to denote the study of climatic, geographical, and social factors that contributed to human diversity. Much early ethnology traced modern peoples back to the descriptions of human development in the Old Testament. In 1843, an Ethnological Society was set up in London as an offshoot of the Aborigines Protection Society. The Quakers who founded this group used it for both philanthropic activism and research: it was intended to draw attention to the abuse of Canadian peoples by the Hudson Bay Company.

In 1863, a new group, calling itself the Anthropological Society, broke away from the Ethnological Society. The new group was much more concerned with the idea of race – and the goal of creating a science of races – than the ethnologists were. It drew influence from the biological sciences rather than geography. Papers on topics such as 'The Negro's Place in Nature' insisted that 'the negro' was 'a distinct species from the European'. Only later was it revealed that James Hunt, who delivered that paper, was in the pay of a leading American pro-slavery campaigner.

The backlash of scientific thinkers against this use of their ideas was immediate. Zoologists, palaeontologists, and other leaders in the biological sciences led an outcry that resulted in the closure of the Anthropological Society, though the term 'anthropology' persisted with the creation of The Royal Anthropological Institute in 1871. In the 1870s, anthropology became closely associated with the scientific study of prehistoric societies and the development of cultures. The word ethnology, on the other hand, fell out of use.

Studies of Victorian anthropology by George Stocking and Robert Young trace the complexities of these developments within scientific circles. But it is striking that the development of ideas of race occurred on a public stage. As the historian of science Sadiah Qureshi has demonstrated, the peoples of empire were regularly 'paraded' in front of British audiences, and racial categories and characterizations were created in interactions between showmen, scientists, and the public. Colonized peoples were regularly exhibited to paying audiences in events that were intended both as entertainment and as lessons. These ranged from small scenes of tribal life in which a family unit might be presented to a ticketed audience by a celebrated showman, to lavish exhibitions that aimed to catalogue whole ways of life. Through advertising and practised showmanship, organizers encouraged viewers to inspect closely the delineations of human difference, analysing what made each 'family of mankind' unique.

John Connolly, for instance, was President of the Ethnological Society in the 1850s. Noting that the 'commercial relations of England' permitted uniquely 'extensive opportunities of intercourse with all the races of men', he used performing groups, including San, Inuit, Zulus, and 'Aztec children', to research the peoples of the world. He championed the systematic study of displayed peoples, insisting that shows were not just 'objects of curiosity or of unfruitful wonder'.

One of the largest exhibits of this kind was Savage South Africa, a lavish show held at Earls Court in 1899. Over two hundred Africans, dozens of Afrikaans, and hundreds of animals were imported as performers. As well as living on-site in a mock African homestead, the Africans re-enacted events of recent history, including the Ndebele War (1893), which still loomed large in British imperial memory.

THE NDEBELE WAR

By the mid-nineteenth century, the Ndebele had established a powerful military state in Matabeleland (now Zimbabwe). European incursions into this area intensified by the 1880s, as imperial agents sought out land and minerals. The leading British player in this contest was Cecil Rhodes, entrepreneur and founder of the De Beers diamond company. In 1888, Rhodes deceptively claimed to have secured the mineral rights to the entire Ndebele kingdom, providing the excuse for a newly formed British South Africa Company to assert its administrative control across the region.

Under the guise of defensive protection, the company set about dismantling Ndebele power by military means. Although the Ndebele were well-trained fighters, the new technology of the Maxim gun (used here for the first time) secured British conquest. The British mistook the temporary defeat of the Ndebele for permanent acceptance of a new colonial order. They failed to recognize the role of military prowess in Ndebele identity or the commitment to the Ndebele that other tribes, chiefly the Shona, still felt. The Ndebele-Shona rebellion of 1896 therefore took them by surprise. By this date, the strategic significance of South Africa was recognized in Parliament and the press, and an Imperial South African Association was founded to 'uphold British supremacy and to promote the interests of British subjects in South Africa'.

Events like Savage South Africa relied on public interest in political and military occurrences to draw in a paying audience. The impresario and organizer, a South African circus owner, narrated the events as a moment in the onward march of progress. A handful of brave, technologically advanced Europeans were seen exerting colonial order amidst hordes of spear- and shield-wielding tribesmen. In this way, the shows did not just create and consolidate scientific or anthropological knowledge, but also encouraged British visitors to support particular readings of imperial history.

An unravelling empire? The second Boer War

Ironically, the initial success of Savage South Africa tailed off when the nation's attention turned to South Africa during the second Boer War. The events of this war were at first conceptualized in terms established in the 1850s: British technological superiority over colonial savagery and the backwardness of other imperial powers. However, this easy confidence did not last long when the British fought Boer settlers armed with weapons that rivalled their own.

From the 1850s, two small states of Dutch-speaking Boer settlers existed precariously amidst British enclaves in Southern Africa. These were not seen as a particularly severe threat to British interests until gold was discovered in one of them, the Transvaal, in 1886. The region's president, Paul Kruger, used his newfound wealth to militarize the Transvaal and seek alliances with European powers. This put him in direct conflict with Cecil Rhodes who, not content with controlling the diamond production of the entire world, founded Consolidated Goldfields of South Africa in 1887. British prospectors soon flooded into the region. The heavy taxes Kruger placed on them, alongside his reluctance to transport goods via British companies in the Cape, were seen by the British as an excuse to meddle in Transvaal affairs.

Rhodes soon began to organize a coup, sanctioned by the British government, to remove Kruger from power. This failed entirely and sparked international censure: a congratulatory telegram sent to Kruger from the German Kaiser raised particular ire among British officials. British citizens in the Transvaal responded by attacking German shops. By the late 1890s, Boer and British interests were in fiercely hostile relations: all that was required was an appropriate moment to launch the long-awaited war.

This crisis posed an ideological problem. Within Britain, defenders of empire tended to present any British military aggression as the defence of missionaries or others engaged in 'civilizing work'; critics of empire presented expansionary activity as greed-driven. In the present crisis, 'civilizing' arguments were not easy to make: more than in any other Victorian conflict the economics of empire were laid bare, stripped of their usual moralizing garb. The Prime Minister, Lord Salisbury, attempted to deploy well-worn rhetoric: 'We seek no gold fields. We seek no territory ... What we desire is equal rights for men of all races'. But this did not command the warm assent that had traditionally greeted such sentiments. Even Sir William Butler, the Commander-in-Chief of British forces in South Africa, felt that British actions were driven by buccaneering capitalism. A leading politician of the next generation, Lloyd George, made his name from impassioned opposition to the war: it was, he insisted, not a matter of freedom but of '45% dividends'.

The result was polarization between critics of empire and exceptionally forceful jingoistic sectors of public opinion, which were soon associated with the phrase 'khaki fever'. When Kruger made his first efforts at expansion into British territory and the British launched their military efforts to depose him, the nationalistic elements of the London press were utterly convinced that the army would land like a hammer-blow on the Transvaal, ending Kruger's experiment almost instantaneously.

However, thanks to a decade of gold extraction, Kruger's militia of farmers was now equipped with Mauser 0.276 rifles, Krupp cannon, and Creusot siege guns. They were better armed than the British, more skilled (especially as marksmen), and better acquainted with the terrain. On the offensive, the Boers won a string of victories and laid siege to both the British army base at Ladysmith and the diamond town of Kimberley (trapping an apoplectic Cecil Rhodes). This forced British forces to split. Thanks to their own strategic errors and the intelligent deployment of Kruger's Boers, setback after setback confronted these depleted armies.

Even when, after committing over 400,000 troops, the British did begin to win victories, they failed to understand the Boer cause and faced intense resistance from 'bitter-enders' long after each victory seemed to be won. The British answered with a scorched earth policy, which disgusted many British soldiers; they also instituted horrific prisoner of war camps, which ended over 20,000 lives and became a precedent for the concentration camps of the twentieth century.

The eventual cost to Britain of the war was estimated at £217 million. Its impact in the British Isles, however, stretched far beyond damage to the public purse. The Boer War instigated a profound crisis of confidence in Britain's imperial 'destiny' and in the vigour of the British 'race'. This gave impetus to a new science: eugenics. Eugenicists aimed to revitalize the 'national stock' through scientifically calculated selective breeding. This rationalistic approach to reproduction, it was argued, could guarantee the robustness of future generations. Nationalistic attempts to shore up British self-confidence confronted deeply pessimistic visions of a degenerating European order. If blithe self-confidence on the international stage was a peculiarly Victorian characteristic, then the Victorian worldview was punctured and destabilized by the events of 1899–1901 but, as another half-century of imperial power attests, it was certainly not destroyed.

5

How cruel time can be: Victorian past, present, and future

> *Suddenly a White Rabbit with pink eyes ran close by her. There was nothing so very remarkable in that; nor did Alice think it so very much out of the way to hear the Rabbit say to itself, 'Oh dear! Oh dear! I shall be late! … but when the Rabbit actually took a watch out of its waistcoat pocket, and looked at it, and then hurried on, Alice started to her feet … just in time to see it pop down a large rabbit-hole under the hedge … The rabbit-hole went straight on like a tunnel for some way, and then dipped suddenly down, so suddenly that Alice had not a moment to think about stopping herself before she found herself falling down a very deep well.*
>
> Lewis Carroll, *Alice in Wonderland* (1865)

Posterity has often been cruel to the Victorians, but time was cruel to them in other ways as well. People often make sense of themselves, and create their own identities, in terms of time as much as place or social status. Who we are is shaped by our vision of where we stand in relation to past and future. Memory and history therefore have powerful roles to play in forming individuals and communities. These facts hit the Victorians hard, because the visions of past, present, and future that were shared at the beginning of the nineteenth century were long dead by its end. They had fallen down a very deep well indeed.

Sciences like geology, astronomy, and evolutionary biology dislodged traditional visions of planetary and human beginnings; at the same time, technology offered seemingly infinite material advance but also posed the question of whether this superficial progress was genuinely beneficial to humanity. The aftermath of the first French Revolution caused thinkers to turn their gaze to past civilizations. The dramatic overthrow of the *ancien regime* had demonstrated the possibility of novel social structures, and the Victorians ransacked the annals of history for alternative visions of the social order. The Victorian era therefore began in a period of crisis and transformation, which demanded new strategies for making sense of the present: new narratives for putting modern Britain in context.

More than any other Britons before (and perhaps after) them, the Victorians made sense of their own world by exploring the societies of the past and endeavouring to understand how the processes of historical change operated. In Thomas Carlyle's words, 'all men are now historians'. Historical consciousness was recognized as a defining characteristic of contemporary Britain by thinkers as divergent as William Gladstone and Friedrich Nietzsche.

In the hands of the Victorians, the Tudor period became the Olden Time, a golden age of community values; ancient Rome provided lessons in good and bad imperialism; ancient Greece was the society in which all the values of the present, whether democracy or militarism, had been invented or moulded into modern forms; ancient Egypt and Mesopotamia, interpreted through the pages of the Old Testament, stood on the boundaries between history and the strange, murky world of prehistory. Stranger still, this prehistory soon yielded an array of weird beasts whose vast skeletons could be seen and touched at the new Natural History Museum: the Victorians were the first people to confront the idea of dinosaurs (a term first used by the palaeontologist Richard Owen in 1842). This total rewriting of time was one of the features of their own age that many Victorians found most unsettling: every shift in interpreting the past or future altered the Victorians' precarious vision of themselves.

If the previous chapters have shown us the Victorians' confident disciplining of space, this chapter shows them at work in a medium in which they were much less confident. And it is crucial to note that this fixation on issues of time was not a characteristic confined to intellectuals or the upper classes. The philosopher of history Peter Fritzsche has expressed this in powerful prose:

> To be cast in the new time of the nineteenth century was to recognise the weird shapes of historical change. Tracing the scars of history … ordinary home dwellers took a passionate, even flamboyant interest in the past.

One reason why these questions affected so many was that a host of great Victorian controversies, in all fields, were essentially chicken-and-egg questions, which made time of paramount importance. Darwinian evolutionists and their opponents argued over whether the world-system was a product of intelligence (a divine creator) or intelligence a product of the world-system (the evolution by natural selection of conscious life); secularists disagreed with defenders of biblical religion over whether Christianity was a product of human values (human cultures made God in their image) or human values a product of Christianity (without religion there would be no morality). Only by exploring the patterns of past and future could the nature of life itself be ascertained.

The past in Parliament

Despite, or perhaps because of, the profoundly democratic nature of discussion of time, this chapter will begin in the House of Commons. This is partly because this book has so far evaded the lofty world of high politics, but also because the roles of time in parliamentary debate are so unexpected. Politicians habitually built their arguments through appeals to history, tradition, and precedent: the distant past was never far away in the Houses of Parliament.

Victorian Parliament was full of men with multiple careers. Many were scholars too, and of these by far the largest number were engaged in historical pursuits. There were, for instance, parliamentarians who were famous for the archaeological excavation of the earliest cities. Austen Henry Layard had an undistinguished youth (he failed to hold down an apprenticeship as a solicitor) before he left Britain in 1839 to seek his fortune in India. Travelling overland, however, he stopped at Mosul (in modern Iraq) and spent the mid-1840s digging up the biblical cities of ancient Mesopotamia. This feat was enough to catapult him into a significant political career, beginning in 1852, during which he continued to develop and publicize his work on the earliest civilizations.

The names of leading historians of England, such as Macaulay or Acton, were prefixed with the title 'Lord': they sat in Parliament's upper house and governed Britain and its colonies according to the principles their works of history proclaimed. Edward Bulwer-Lytton was a parliamentary mover-and-shaker who changed parties and political roles on multiple occasions. He also wrote numerous historical novels, including a blockbusting romance, *The Last Days of Pompeii* (1836), which anatomized the different historical characteristics of Greek, Roman, Egyptian, and Christian peoples. Odder still, William Gladstone, a man with one of the busiest political careers of the century, published more pages on the ancient poet Homer than did any other nineteenth-century writer.

THE HOUSES OF PARLIAMENT

- The British Parliament is made up of two houses: the Commons and the Lords. The House of Commons consists of elected members of Parliament. The House of Lords consists of hereditary and appointed peers.

- The Commons is now firmly associated with party politics. There are three main parties: Conservatives are associated with centre-right ideologies; Labour is associated with left-leaning politics; and the Liberal Democrats are associated with a more 'centrist' position. Each MP is expected to vote with their party on key issues. This system is a product of changes made during the Victorian period.
- At the beginning of the Victorian period, the House of Commons was very different. Party politics was only just emerging as the interests of groups of MPs began to coalesce into two units: Whigs and Tories. These groupings were fragile (the Tories had a particularly dramatic split in 1846, for instance) and many MPs moved between parties. There were also smaller groupings, including Radicals, Irish MPs, and Peelites. These parties cannot easily be interpreted in terms of 'left' and 'right': the spatial metaphors we use to make sense of political ideologies simply do not map onto the nineteenth-century system.
- In the 1840s, a new power bloc began to form from an alliance of Whigs, Radicals, and free-trade Peelites. In 1859, this was named the Liberal Party. The later Victorian decades were dominated by an increasingly formalized conflict between Liberals and Conservatives. Two huge personalities, Gladstone (Liberal, four-times Prime Minister) and Disraeli (Conservative, twice Prime Minister), dominated the political landscape. In 1900, the Labour Party was founded as a political pressure group. By this stage, the parliamentary system was beginning to take the institutional and ideological shapes that are recognizable today.

Politicians treated history as a catalogue of past decisions made by leaders whose triumphs or mistakes could provide guidance for the diplomats and statesmen of the present. Alongside this, a peculiarly Victorian mode of thought insisted that to describe the origins of something was the same as explaining it. In this way, people were not just fascinated by beginnings; they also believed that analysing origins would allow them to understand the nature of the present. The quest for origins was an effort to comprehend current circumstances: it was conducted by the trailblazing early Victorian geologists, Darwinian evolutionary scientists, anthropologists who studied 'primitive man', archaeologists who explored Stonehenge and the pyramids, the eminent Lords who assessed the beginnings of Britain's constitution, or the many Victorians who practised the art of autobiography.

These strong links drawn between past and present were often stated explicitly. The historian Edward Freeman, for instance, began his 1870s lectures on the Germanic peoples of the early centuries AD by stating that his aim was 'to prove that the English are English'. Freeman had a particular agenda to pursue in defining modern 'Englishness' and believed he could demonstrate its validity by tracing the ancient origins of his pet idea.

Victorian politicians often believed strongly in their own significance in history: high politics, they believed, was where history happened. Considering themselves the chosen few of a chosen race, they endeavoured to discover their own purpose by looking to the beginnings of the processes of which they saw themselves a part. George Grote, a leading radical MP, saw himself as a firebrand in the cause of democracy, so he analysed the invention and development of democratic principles, tying himself into two millennia of history. Gladstone was riddled with anxiety concerning the relationship between religion and secular society in the modern world. He saw himself as an agent for reconciling and uniting the two, so he obsessed over the relationships between the Old Testament and the Homeric poems. When Victorian politicians such as Macaulay wrote history, they usually presented 'great men' – people they saw as their own precursors – making the momentous decisions that caused progressive historical development.

Although history could provide opportunities for self-congratulation, showing how moderns were better than the people of the past and demonstrating just how far the Victorians had come from the dark days of previous generations, age could also make things venerable and respectable.

This was the reasoning behind the construction of the modern Houses of Parliament, built between 1840 and 1867 in the style of an elaborate medieval and Tudor fantasy. From Big Ben to the classic view of Parliament from the Thames, this new 'Palace of Westminster' was designed by Charles Barry and Augustus Welby Pugin to look half a millennium old and thereby convey all the authority of a venerable tradition.

GOTHIC REVIVAL

- Gothic buildings built between the twelfth and sixteenth centuries became a major source of inspiration for Victorian architects and designers. They associated these buildings, particularly English cathedrals, with a golden age of craftsmanship and community ideals. This was in part a reaction against machine production, the generic appearance of factories, and other consequences of the industrial revolution.
- This medieval architecture was considered peculiarly 'English' or Anglo-German ('Teutonic') as opposed to alternative Greek or Italianate styles. It conjured medieval chivalry and romance, which also became an ideal for social behaviour, particularly the relationships between men and women. In the contrast between Gothic and Greek, a whole range of contrasting political and religious ideas were encoded. Supporters of Gothic architecture were more likely to be conservative in their politics and Catholic in their religious leanings (although this was not always true).
- Gothic style was characterized by pointed arches, intricate decoration, airy spaces, tall windows, and elaborate stained glass. It was later associated with Arts and Crafts furniture and tapestry such as that designed by William Morris.
- John Ruskin was a major champion of the Gothic Revival. He associated Greek architecture with slavery and Gothic architecture with free, skilled craftsmen. Ruskin also supported the medievalism of painters such as the Pre-Raphaelites.
- The fiercest advocate of Gothic architecture was Augustus Welby Pugin, subject of an accomplished and compelling biography (Rosemary Hill's *God's Architect*). To Pugin, Greek or Roman styles were 'pagan'. They offended not just against the laws of beauty but also against the laws of morality. Only a Roman Catholic society, he argued, could produce a wholesome architecture in the true medieval style.

This Gothic Revival stretched far beyond Westminster. The architectural historian Charles Delheim summed up the enormous impact of Gothicism in architecture: 'London in 1900 was more medieval than at any time since 1666.' Paradoxically, it was those buildings that represented the greatest break with the past that were given the most insistently medieval dress. London's most ferociously modern transport hub, St Pancras Station, was cathedral-like and medieval, stressing in its outward appearance a continuity that its function belied. It is no coincidence that Alice Chandler's book on Victorian medievalism is entitled *A Dream of Order*: the medieval could often be a comfort blanket. It was rarely a nostalgic rejection of change, but a reassuring demonstration that the transformation of some aspects of life – the advent of the railways or of democracy – did not destroy continuity in others.

History and tyranny

It is only by looking back to the aftermath of the American, French, and Haitian revolutions, and exploring the historical meanings of democracy itself, that we can comprehend why Parliament was infused with historical thought at the start of the Victorian period. Democracy was once a very dirty word. Aristotle had considered the term to describe (as one Victorian commentator paraphrased him) 'the most debased form of a republic'. Similarly negative connotations surrounded the concept throughout the early nineteenth century. Alongside this, the monarchical rule that defined *ancien regime* states had not been understood to be just one among several kinds of possible political order; it was thought of as the only divinely sanctioned system. It was commensurate with civilization itself: to be ruled by anything other than a monarch and a fiendishly complex aristocratic structure was to be uncivilized. The American and French revolutions in 1776 and 1789 did far more than overturn the political order of two nations. By creating a new structure that did away with kingship, they shattered conceptions about what was 'natural' and 'preordained' in politics. They made the investigation of alternative forms of social order not just desirable but necessary, and they undermined the principle that there was only one possible way to rule a modern state.

After the revolutions, a great deal of the debate that redefined the term democracy and analysed the options available to a nation was conducted through histories of ancient Greece. These pitted Sparta, standing for the rule of the powerful few – oligarchy – against Athens, representing the rule of the many. By the early nineteenth century, when social inequality and unrest meant that the political future of Britain was balanced on a knife edge, the idea of a close relationship between the political histories of ancient Greece and modern Britain had become an almost unquestioned assumption among politicians and intellectuals.

Opponents of reform wielded Sparta as a glorious example of powerful leaders, unfettered by the opinions of lesser mortals, acting in the interests of their state. Reformers, on the other hand, presented Athens as the product of enlightened commitment to equality and general prosperity. The leading political economist of the age, John Stuart Mill, was not being particularly controversial when he stated that 'the battle of Marathon, even as an event in English history, is more important than the battle of Hastings'. What was at stake when Athens confronted Persia at Marathon in 490BC were the big ideas that defined many parliamentary agendas: Citizenship, Liberty, Law, Civilization, and, eventually, Democracy.

The major text on the history of Greece that shaped early nineteenth-century attitudes was begun in the decade before the French Revolution but its tenth and final volume was only completed in 1810. Victorian historians often praised this work as the first to 'find out that Grecian history was a living thing with a practical bearing'. In the words of Frank Turner, author of *The Greek Heritage in Victorian Britain* (1981), that history 'legitimised the use of Athenian history as a vehicle for debating ... the wisdom and viability of modern democratic government'.

This *History of Greece* was written by William Mitford, a Hampshire country gentleman and member of Parliament who despised the very idea of democracy. Turner shows how Mitford's volumes on Greece 'were a panegyric ... on the virtues of the balanced English constitution and a polemic against those who would undermine that balance in the name of democracy, the people, or antique precedents'. Those in America, France, and at home who wanted to transform the modern world in the image of ancient republics were simply wrongheaded: they could no more secure long-term stability than the Greek states had.

Mitford told the story of Greece as a narrative of decline from the balanced monarchies described in the earliest Greek texts, particularly Homer's *Iliad*, into multiple forms of republic including Sparta and Athens. Some republics were weaker than others, but all were mere shadows of the grand monarchical originals. Mitford explained the inadequacies of the Athenian republic by arguing that the evil of slavery was directly linked to democracy: only because slaves kept Athenian society running could free citizens (that deluded 'community of lordly beggars') spend time conducting government.

As late as 1819, Mitford's celebration of 'the wisdom of tyranny' could seem to have been penned in 'the true English spirit'. By the beginning of the Victorian period, it seemed itself to belong to ancient times. Burgeoning pressure for reform and large-scale reaction against aristocratic corruption meant that a new vision of Greece was required for a new political ideology. Greek tyrants and kings were soon presented as rapacious men whose only interest was in keeping the fruits of misgovernment for themselves. Democracy, for the first time in British history, was becoming an ideal to aspire towards.

History and democracy

The backlash against Mitford was led by a young city banker called George Grote who soon became the leading radical agitator in Parliament. Grote was associated with a particular milieu, known as the 'philosophical radicals', who published their opinions in a progressive journal called the *Westminster Review*. This group associated its ideals with the foundation of England's first university to accept non-Anglicans, 'the godless institution of Gower Street', University College London. They carried out their democratic agitation under the influence of the social reformer Jeremy Bentham, whose preserved body still sits in the south cloister of the college. Leading philosophical radicals included Edwin Chadwick, who would campaign for improved sanitation in London, the utopian socialist Robert Owen, and the leading political economist of the age John Stuart Mill. This makes a prestigious roll call of progressive Victorian thought.

Bentham's principles, favoured by many of the philosophical radicals, began from ideals of individual freedom, whether economic, legal, intellectual, political, or sexual. The years 1833 (after the first wave of parliamentary reform) to 1840 were the heyday of the philosophical radicals, and it was after they lost much of their parliamentary power in the election of 1840 that George Grote turned from direct political agitation to make an extended intellectual case for radical principles.

It was entirely in keeping with the spirit of the age that the cases for democracy, liberty, and reform should achieve their greatest statement in a vast historical survey of an ancient society. Grote's twelve-volume *History of Greece* (1846–56), even more than Mitford's books, showed that anything a British writer wrote about Athens they actually wrote about Britain. Grote praised the Athenians in effusive terms: a reformed House of Commons, he suggested, would, and should, look just like the ancient Athenian Assembly.

Athenian leaders, Grote insisted, were the ancient equivalents of modern progressive thinkers. Their mastery of the arts of governance was such that they were able to devote unique resources to social and individual improvement. The result was that their society saw an astonishing outpouring of art, philosophy, and the political innovations that could secure individual liberty. As Frank Turner noted, 'after the appearance of Grote's *History of Greece* Englishmen looked at the Athenians and saw in large measure the reflection of their own best selves'. What it meant to be English, Scottish, Welsh, Irish, or British was now frequently conceived as what it meant to be a direct philosophical descendant of Athens.

In the specific terms of Grote's celebration of Athens, the ideals of the early Victorian liberal reformers were set out in detail. These included government by consent, freedom of discussion, public responsibility of leaders and officials, due process in legal affairs, equality before the law, security of property and person, and rigorous political checks and balances to prevent corruption and the abuse of power.

Between 1832 and 1928, Britain was transformed into a society that could be called democratic. What Mitford, Grote, and the hundreds of others who wrote about ancient Athens did was to produce the precise understanding of what democracy meant that could then be transferred to the political context of the present day. Only later in the century, as new reformers sought to nudge the education system away from the classics towards engineering and the sciences, was the dark side of Athenian politics – particularly its dependence on slavery – returned to the agenda. Only in the closing decades of the Victorian era were Greece and Rome cast off as models for modernity.

Into the deep: Victorian prehistories

Although the appropriation of Greece and Rome was diverse and sometimes deeply subversive, they were widely considered to be the possessions of the political elite. Grote may have been a radical, but from 1833 onwards he was a radical within the political establishment. Tests in Latin and Greek were one way among many by which class privilege was sustained, ensuring that the working classes and non-Anglicans (excluded from the Latin and Greek training of exclusive public schools and the established universities) were kept out of many prestigious posts, including the higher reaches of colonial administration. One result of this was that those who wished to rival the establishment chose rival histories. In the 1820s and 30s, for instance, Methodist and Baptist leaders in Newcastle chose ancient Egypt as their history of choice. Treating Greece as a society of pampered pontificators (with parallels to the worlds of aloof Home Counties aristocrats and complacent Church of England clergymen), they praised the engineering prowess of the pyramid builders, whose achievements in stone provided inspiration for the architectural challenges of the industrial age.

The pre-classical civilizations of Egypt and Mesopotamia were known primarily from the Bible; it was in the nineteenth century that their scripts (hieroglyphs and cuneiform) were deciphered and the first texts translated. Victorians assumed that these texts would have direct bearing on the Old Testament. Some thought their contents might 'prove' or 'disprove' biblical events, but for the most devout these texts would simply serve to illustrate the lives of the people of the Bible and make this intensely Christian society more knowledgeable concerning its own religion. The new sciences of Egyptology and Assyriology were therefore treated with both intense excitement and great fear. Ancient history, it seemed, could either validate or destroy the most cherished values and origin narratives of Protestant Britain. As the century wore on, biblical cities such as Nineveh were excavated, although expectations that archaeology would reveal material with direct and irrefutable bearing on the Bible were always frustrated.

The deeper back in time this knowledge carried the Victorians, the more exhilarating and controversial it became.

The origins of ancient Egypt were one focus of debate. Egypt's greatest achievements, such as the pyramids and sphinx, seemed to come from the very beginning of its history: these monuments were widely assumed to be the oldest constructed objects in the world. The fact that the first humans seemed capable of architectural feats that would stretch the limits of modern industry posed many questions about the nature of progress. Many Victorians used this term – progress – as both a tool for interpreting the world and a rallying cry for the future, so anything that seemed to challenge their narrative of inexorable, accelerating improvement was a focus for intense speculation. Egypt seemed to suggest that the origins of humanity were in a golden age of high civilization rather than an era of unsophisticated barbarism. By the late nineteenth century, Egypt had become a favourite theme of anti-Darwinian writers who defended the idea that the world was millions rather than billions of years old.

However, the building of the pyramids and the beginnings of Egyptian history were relatively recent compared to the most powerful scientific concerns of the age. This was the period when the scale of time became unimaginable, only to be grasped by metaphors. The relation of human history to the world's total past was that of a fingernail to an outstretched arm; it was a layer of paint on the summit of the Eiffel Tower; it was the blink of an eye within a human lifetime.

All three of the most prestigious sciences of the period were entangled with the dizzying new idea of deep time. Astronomers asked how and when had the stars and planets formed. They came up with theories such as the nebular hypothesis, which suggested slow formation over billions of years. They realized that, because of the finite speed of light, their telescopes observed distant objects as they had existed millions of years ago: astronomy was the only discipline that could *actually see* the past. Geologists found the skills to turn rocks into an archive of prehistory similar to the archives of texts read by historians. The great innovation in the life sciences was the realization that species of animals and plants had histories no less than nations or royal dynasties. All three sciences provided huge vistas on a prehuman world that was as eventful and exciting as any battle a historian might record. All three made humans seem like small distractions at the margins of a vast cosmic order rather than the focal point of a system designed especially for them.

What was most striking about this scientific fervour was its intense popular appeal. As the historian of science James Secord has noted:

> For the first time in history, the consequences of a scientific understanding were being developed not just for wealthy and privileged elites, but for a wide range of men and women, particularly in the middle classes and upper reaches of the working population.

Writers on science coveted the ideal of mass scientific literacy. Many of their works in the early Victorian period were far more than scientific texts. They advocated particular kinds of behaviour. These books were gripping guides to a way of life that was formed around the heroic pursuit of knowledge; they were philosophical conduct manuals as much as specialized textbooks.

No science felt more urgent and challenging for many early Victorians than geology. This new practice was always read in the context of philosophical and theological debates: to say anything about the origins and development of the earth was to say something, too, about the narrative of Genesis in the Old Testament. The Creation story had to be confronted by every geologist (when audiences expected this confrontation, even refusing to write about it was a kind of confrontation). The response each geologist chose defined the reception of their work: the circulation and impact of geological texts was related closely to their perceived 'moral' purpose.

One example of this can be found in the work of the extraordinary Oxford eccentric William Buckland, one of the leading geologists of the early Victorian decades. Buckland was renowned for his endeavour to further scientific knowledge by eating every species of animal on earth. The famous blue bag he carried with him might hold hyena skulls or fossilized faeces to be wielded at the unsuspecting colleagues with whom he dined. Behind this buffoonery (of which earnest thinkers of the next generation, including Darwin, deeply disapproved) was an approach to geology that left space for scripture. To Buckland, the biblical flood had been the last in a series of geological catastrophes that had gouged the troughs and peaks of the modern landscape. Geology and the Bible were part of a single explanation for the development of human society. Buckland's most famous text, *Geology and Mineralogy* (1836), was part of a series of treatises funded by a bequest from the Earl of Bridgewater for scholarly works attesting to 'the Power, Wisdom, and Goodness of God as manifested in the Creation'.

Buckland was once interpreted as a conservative biblical apologist whose work suffered because of his fixation on the Book of Genesis. As recent historians of science have shown, this is not a helpful interpretation. Buckland's geological discoveries were profound and progressive: he simply operated in the world of early nineteenth-century Britain, where the distinctions between theology and science remained porous and indistinct. The key figures in establishing these boundaries and creating modern definitions of the natural sciences were still at the beginnings of their careers. These include the geologist Charles Lyell, whose *Principles of Geology* (1830) became the foundational text of Victorian geology. Lyell's careful work on the formation of landmasses and, later, on the relationship of human remains to those of extinct creatures was trailblazing. In the 1860s and 70s, however, this geologist who had done so much to remove theological influence from geological science was a key opponent of Darwin's vision of human evolution. The relationships between science and religion in the construction of deep time remained more complex than is often assumed.

'The unique predominance of the present time?'

Among historical civilizations, a few – ancient Greece, Rome, the Tudors, and the English seventeenth century – dominated the historical thinking of the early and mid-Victorian periods. After 1870, the influence of these periods lost their power as models for the present. This has been described as giving way to a *fin de siècle* culture that abandoned historical reference in favour of a unique, pervasive focus on the present.

FIN DE SIÈCLE

- This phrase is used to denote changes in British culture from c.1880 onwards. It evokes the gradual abandonment of tastes considered Victorian and the beginnings of trends that would lead to modernism in the arts.
- In art and literature, the idea of a *fin de siècle* was associated with the 'art of shocking', with dandyism, overt sexuality, and drug taking.
- Two artistic movements – decadence and aestheticism – embodied a *fin de siècle* rejection of morality and virtue as the most important things in life, embracing beauty and even decay in their place. Max Nordau's *Degeneration* (1894, published first in German as *Entartung*, 1892) famously identified and condemned the ideals of these movements.
- Another famous book, Holbrook Jackson's *The Eighteen Nineties* (1922), provided a more sympathetic and more elegant treatment of the age.
- Many of the best-loved Victorians, including Oscar Wilde, were figureheads of *fin de siècle* aestheticism. They took a more detached, often ironic, attitude to issues of public propriety that makes them seem much more 'modern' than figures from just a few years before.

This analysis captures something, but not quite what it claims to. What was going on was a diversification of historical interests that had previously been intense and focused. Both the volume of writing on historical themes and the range of historical settings that were written about continued to grow. New interest arose in histories from ancient China to medieval Persia and the classical civilizations of Central America. A range of 'neo-' trends, from Neo-Assyrian to Neo-Byzantine, Egyptian, and Aztec, proliferated in architecture. These provided diverse new historical models, but they also fuelled concerns that British culture had lost its core: that society had become so diverse that there was no longer anything holding it together. The volume of writing on Greece and Rome also rose, although it would never again be integrated into public life as it was in the middle of the century. What was lost after 1870 was the sense that these historical settings had direct relevance for present-day politics.

As the political historian Duncan Bell has argued in an article entitled 'From Ancient to Modern in Victorian Imperial Thought', appeals to precedent and tradition lost much of their persuasive power in this period. Political thinkers looked increasingly to the American present as a model for the future. The federal nature of American politics seemed to offer a model for British 'imperial federation' in which Australia, New Zealand, and Canada would remain part of 'Greater Britain'.

Equally significantly, amidst signs of declining British fortunes, thinkers attempted to distance Britain from the cycles of rise and fall that seemed to characterize the empires of the ancient world. The British Empire, they insisted, was a phenomenon 'without precedent in the past'. As J.R. Seeley put it in *The Expansion of England* (1884), 'our colonies do not resemble the colonies which classical students meet with in Greek and Roman history, and our Empire is not an Empire at all in the ordinary sense of the word'.

Britain was no longer seen as the New Rome or the New Athens, but a unique political development not bound by any 'laws' derived from history. The recent example of the United States was the closest thing to a model. It was the only proof that 'immense territorial' expansion 'is not incompatible ... with that representative system of government which had its birth and development in England, and its most notable adaptation in America'.

If America offered one vision of the future, an increasing range of other options were explored at the close of the century. Some of these were dystopian visions of all that could go wrong in society's development; others offered up utopian visions of an ideal future. Many were conducted in literary sketches of imagined future worlds, which aimed to teach new politics or new attitudes to science. They provide unique insights into Victorian hopes, fears, and eccentricities.

In *News from Nowhere* (1890), the leading socialist and designer William Morris fused his politics with the medieval romance tradition. The protagonist tours a future society with no private property, no cities, and no criminals, which is held together by pastoral love of the land. He meets along the way a host of characters, each drawn from the romance tradition but teaching a modern socialist philosophy.

Looking Backward, 2000–1887 (1887) was written by a Massachusetts lawyer, Edward Bellamy, and became an immediate bestseller in Britain. Like Morris's protagonist, Bellamy's character finds himself in a socialist utopia of the future (the year 2000). Although property here is also nationalized, this is a different utopia from that depicted by Morris: it is not agricultural but industrial. This society differs from the nineteenth century in the respect it affords labourers: working hours are short and all workers retire aged forty-five. Like Morris, Bellamy makes every difference between the world in which he is writing and the imaginary world he describes into a criticism of the social and economic organization of the present.

Not all socialist depictions of the future came in utopian or dystopian novels. Other socialists penned long poems.

For instance, Edward Carpenter's *Towards Democracy* and *Love's Coming of Age* aimed to persuade society towards a new world of social and sexual freedom. Some, including Carpenter, established rural communes in which this vision of the future might be pursued in practice.

Many visions of the future were in fact early science fiction stories, known at first as 'scientific romances'. There are earlier stories in this genre, including the works of Jules Verne, but the 1890s saw the genre popularized and many of its most significant texts produced. Some tales explored the possibilities of life on other planets, particularly Mars and Venus. H.G. Wells's *War of the Worlds*, with its Martian conquest of earth, was published in 1897; by that year, the genre was popular enough to be parodied by the naval authority (and founder of Jane's Information Group) Fred Jane in *To Venus in Five Seconds*.

Much 1890s sci-fi explores the social and ethical impact of scientific inventions. In some, the scientist becomes the saviour of humanity, producing almost miraculous innovations to escape the threats the future brings. In others, scientific arrogance, and pursuit of progress at all costs, is the cause of those threats. Wells's *The Island of Doctor Moreau* (1896), for instance, recalled Mary Shelley's *Frankenstein* (1818) in its vision of the creation of human-like life in the laboratory; it proved inspirational for early anti-vivisection campaigners.

However, it was not always the scientist who was the focal point of science fiction narratives. In 1898, Wells serialized a story called 'When the Sleeper Wakes', later published as the novel *The Sleeper Awakes* (1910). In this dystopian tale, a Victorian called Graham sleeps for 203 years because of drugs he has taken to cure insomnia. He awakes in a horrifying new London. Two centuries of accumulating interest on Graham's trust fund has made him the richest man in the world, but a sinister organization, the White Council, has been using his wealth to establish a new global order. They had never expected Graham, legally the owner of the entire globe, to awake. As the premise of this tale hints, Victorian interest in the future was often not scientific but economic in nature.

Many late Victorians saw themselves less as descendants of Athens, more as economic trend-setters for the societies of the future. European observers often agreed. According to the French novelist Stendhal, Britain was 'the mirror of our future' in which 'scenes of future life' could be discerned. Particular economic developments, however, made predicting and controlling the future a new obsession. A product of this was the London Stock Exchange, built in 1801 (stocks had previously been traded in London coffee houses). It expanded rapidly. 'Railway Mania' soon led banks to lend on an unprecedented scale so that people could invest in railway shares. Many buyers were defrauded; some individuals, such as 'the railway king' George Hudson, made a fortune from dishonest trading. It was said of such speculators that they gambled not only on the future but on the hereafter, jeopardizing their souls by exploiting the trust of others. Later in the century, the gradual development of the telegraph made long-distance communication almost instantaneous and thereby created trading possibilities on a new scale. The result was a Royal Commission in 1877 charged to ascertain whether, in the possibilities it offered to the unscrupulous, the stock exchange was flawed beyond repair.

Stabilizing the stock market meant making the future predictable. Financial discourse used words such as 'augury', 'prophecy', and 'prediction' in its discussion of how future manias and panics might be predicted and prevented. As D. Morier Evans put it in his 1859 work *History of the Commercial Crisis 1857–8 and the Stock Exchange Panic of 1859*:

> Within the last sixty years, at comparatively short intervals, the commercial world has been disturbed by a succession of these terrible convulsions … familiar to every ear by

> the expressive name, 'panic' ... all have resembled each other in occurring immediately after a period of apparent prosperity, the hollowness of which it has exposed. So uniform is this sequence, that whenever we find ourselves under circumstances that enable the acquisition of rapid fortunes ... we may almost be justified in auguring that the time for panic is at hand.

As the complexity of the economy increased, politicians, financiers, and journalists traced the course of historical crashes in the hope that they could use history to predict and control the future.

In this way, Victorians continued to use the past to make sense of present and future. By the 1890s, this was no longer conducted through vast philosophical histories of ancient Greece, but Carlyle's dictum that 'all men are historians' was no less true. Indeed, Carlyle saw his own history writing as a form of prophecy. He might have added that all people were now historians because rapid socio-economic change caused them to seek methods of interpreting the future. It is no coincidence that the best-known creator of Victorian visions of the future, H.G. Wells, also wrote the bestselling history book of the early twentieth century: *The Outline of History: Being a Plain History of Life and Mankind* (1919). In the introduction, Wells wrote:

> The history of mankind ... is a history of more or less blind endeavours to conceive a common purpose in relation to which all men may live happily, and to create and develop a common stock of knowledge which may serve and illuminate that purpose.

Exploring the past, like predicting the future, was a way of attempting to transform 'blind endeavours' into clear-sighted advance.

6

A community of believers? Religion in Victorian Britain

Be this then forever before us; be our first thought morning by morning to think of the resurrection; be our last night by night, the sleep of death, after which cometh the judgement ... remember the parching flame, the never-dying worm, the everlasting fire, the gnashing of teeth, the smoke of torment which goeth up for ever and ever ... Set God before your eye, so you may escape hell, and by God's mercy attain heaven.

Edward Pusey, *The Day of Judgement* (1839)

Religion played an intense and pervasive role in Victorian worldviews. Belief was not something incidental to everyday life but a framework in which literature, science, politics, and life itself took place. Even those Victorians who were furthest from the dominant Christian orthodoxy professed some form of belief or expressed their unbelief in terms riddled with biblical reference and spiritual ideas. As Timothy Larsen has shown in a study aptly called *A People of One Book* (2012), the Jewish and Christian Bibles were a foreground clamour or a background hum to every debate in Victorian Britain.

This extraordinary status for religion amounts to one of the biggest differences between Victorian society and modern Britain. Thinking ourselves into a world bounded by heaven and hell, mediated by politically powerful established churches, where books on religion were published by the million and circulated through every social station and continent of the globe, is a significant task for anyone who wishes to understand the Victorians.

The late eighteenth-century Enlightenment is often presented as a key moment in the decline of religion in Britain. Nothing could be further from the truth. In fact, the Victorian period began in the midst of one of the most intense religious revivals in history. The evangelical revival, which swept across Britain at the end of the eighteenth century and held sway into the middle of the nineteenth, transformed British culture. According to the leading historian of evangelicalism Boyd Hilton, around a third of early Victorians could be called evangelicals, but this revival shaped the lives and thought even of those who were not.

One of evangelicalism's hallmarks was a fixation on the reality of heaven and hell. This conviction that nonbelievers would suffer eternal torment after death led to an urgent need to save souls. A deeply serious outlook on life could result from this, sometimes scorning not just alcohol but most forms of entertainment. Atonement both for sins committed and for the inherently sinful nature of humanity became the priority of many evangelical lives. The early nineteenth century has therefore been called 'the age of atonement'.

Also characteristic of the evangelical outlook was a belief in a direct relationship with God and an intense focus on scripture. Biblical truths were not to be mediated by priests, but interpreted in the communion between the individual conscience and a deeply personal deity. In *The Age of Atonement* (1988), Hilton showed how the economic logic on which nineteenth-century society was built was a product of the distinctive evangelical worldview. No area of society – from the sciences to high politics – escaped the grip of the evangelical ethic. Shaping various religious groups – including the Church of England but also Methodists, Baptists, and many others – evangelicalism was a pervasive mood and set of ethical principles rather than an aspect of a particular religious denomination.

THE SCOTTISH CHURCHES

Anglicanism was the established church in England and (for official purposes at least) in Wales and Ireland. The Presbyterian Church fulfilled the equivalent role in Scotland. Scotland rejected Roman Catholic authority under the influence of a Scottish follower of John Calvin, John Knox (1505–72). A century later, Scotland fought for religious independence once again: 'Covenanters' undertook an armed insurrection to prevent Anglican worship being imposed on Scotland. The Act of Union in 1707 guaranteed religious 'devolution': the Scottish Presbyterian Church remained independent.

The term 'Presbyterian' refers to a particular mode of church government by representative assemblies of church elders. The theology of Scottish Presbyterians was Calvinist. This implies stern emphasis on the absolute authority of God and the scriptures, as well as the necessity of grace through faith in Christ. In the nineteenth century, the regulative practice of worship (the principle that anything not commanded in church was forbidden) prevented many Presbyterian churches from singing hymns or featuring music of any kind. Presbyterian meeting houses (not usually called churches) were typically plain, without stained glass, elaborate decoration, or images.

The early Victorian period was a tumultuous time for the Scottish Church. The period 1834–43 is known as the Ten Years' Conflict, which ended in the Great Disruption. Some Presbyterians wished to ally the Church with landed and political interests (like the Church–state relationship in England), while others wished to retain absolute autonomy. In the Great Disruption, 474 of 1,200 Presbyterian ministers insisted on autonomy. They left the church and founded the Free Church of Scotland. Led by the charismatic moral philosopher Thomas Chalmers, the members of the 'wee free' church insisted on the sovereignty of the church within its own domain.

Revivalism had diverse effects in different parts of Britain. The Anglican Church had an official presence in Wales, but this could not minister to Welsh agricultural and manufacturing workers who continued to vigorously champion evangelical dissenting sects, particularly Methodism. Scotland had its own Presbyterian Church, which was itself split apart when the 'Great Disruption' of 1843 resulted in the foundation of the Free Church of Scotland. Much of Northern England, as well as the mining regions of Cornwall, had more in common with Wales or Scotland than with Anglican heartlands in the South East. The biggest gulf, however, existed between the overwhelmingly Protestant British mainland and Catholic Ireland. The intensity of evangelical Protestantism meant that, even after Catholic Emancipation in 1829, Protestant opinion could be fiercely anti-Catholic (evangelicals were divided on whether Catholics would end up in heaven or hell). The mid-century featured as much anti-Catholic discrimination as had the decades when Britain was at war with Catholic France.

Early Victorian religiosity was hardly likely to maintain so extravagant an intensity for long. The subsequent cooling of religious enthusiasm has often been identified as the beginning of a long-term process of secularization, making mass agnosticism and atheism possible and pointing towards a future without religion. Phrases such as 'Crisis of Faith' and 'Age of Doubt' are frequently applied to this period. They indicate the religious self-scrutiny of several high-profile figures such as Thomas Carlyle and Matthew Arnold. Many of these did lose their commitment to religious orthodoxy. For instance, they no longer believed in the literal truth of the Book of Genesis. Yet very few abandoned faith altogether. Indeed, another book by Larsen, *The Crisis of Doubt*, has shown how the religious crises of famous doubters were usually resolved not in unbelief but in commitment to beliefs that were not all that far from Christian orthodoxy.

The second half of the nineteenth century *was* a period of secularization. But secularization was something quite different from what common understanding of the term suggests. Before the twentieth century, secularization did not mean that large numbers of people ceased to be religious. It simply implied that religion began to play a different, often less public, role in their lives. The primary meanings of secularization for this period relate to an increasing privatization of belief and the separation of Church and state. Paradoxically, these two forms of secularization were deliberately pushed forward by many of the most religious people in society. This included devout Methodists and Baptists who did not believe the Church of England should have exclusive access to political power. Secularization, in this way, was a religious project.

The democratization of nineteenth-century society was accompanied by gradual acceptance of religious freedoms. Where Catholics and Jews had been denied access to parliamentary politics until the 1820s, there were Catholic, Jewish, Muslim, and atheist MPs and peers by the end of the period. The established universities, Oxford and Cambridge, were among the slowest to adapt. Until 1856, no student could be admitted who did not sign up to all 'thirty-nine articles', which set out the distinctive beliefs of the Church of England. Only after 1871 could non-Anglicans teach in these universities.

THE THIRTY-NINE ARTICLES

Established in 1562, the thirty-nine articles summarized the beliefs of the Church of England.

Article I required Anglicans to believe in the Holy Trinity; Article IX insisted on the doctrine of Original Sin, 'the fault and corruption of the nature of every man'; Article XVIII decreed that this sinfulness could only be undone by the Name of Jesus Christ; Article XIX decreed that the churches of the Roman Catholic and Orthodox Churches had erred.

Anglicans were required by the thirty-nine articles to believe in hell but not purgatory and to agree that the scriptures contained all knowledge required for salvation.

New freedoms had important implications. One of the most significant stories of the Victorian period was the success of dissenting denominations. These were, like the Church of England, Protestant. They had split from the Church over various matters of faith in the course of three centuries. Some of the resulting denominations – including Methodists, Baptists, and Congregationalists – grew at a phenomenal rate in industrial and manufacturing regions where official Church structures failed to keep up with a booming population. By the late Victorian period, many dissenting preachers such as the London Baptist minister Charles Spurgeon, known as 'the apostle of the grocers', were celebrities on a national scale.

One implication of this, which many Anglicans found deeply shocking, was that the Church of England no longer represented the nation in any straightforward way. Even the most conservative were forced to recognize that there was competition in religion, which echoed the dynamics of the marketplace. In this world of religious choice, it became possible to profess any belief or no belief at all. The late Victorian period was characterized by a proliferation of spiritual options, what Jose Harris has called 'a cacophony of inner beliefs', rather than a process of growing unbelief.

Low, High, or Broad?

The religious landscape of the nineteenth century was bewilderingly complex, in part because religious denominations had a tendency to split at the slightest sign of disagreement. The Methodist denomination alone had fragmented into dozens of groups by mid-century. Large subdivisions such as Wesleyan Methodists and Calvinist Methodists were divided by substantive theological disagreements; Primitive Methodists broke away in part because of their special commitment to women preachers; Forest Methodists practised a folkish outdoors religion dubbed 'Magic Methodism' by its critics. Some of these divisions were based on class antagonisms: working-class revivalism produced distinctive forms of religion in manufacturing and mining districts.

The picture is further complicated by the fact that many movements, including evangelicalism itself, did not operate within denominations but cut across them. There is still no single book that sets out the beliefs and identities of the many religious groups of the period (what is needed, perhaps, is an encyclopaedia of Victorian religion). There are, however, several terms used by the Victorians that can help delineate the axis of disagreement both within the established churches and among their competitors.

Anglicanism was a surprisingly resilient force throughout the century. Thought to be in crisis at its outset, and failing to cope with urbanization and industrialization in the early Victorian decades, a programme of massive spending and urban expansion resulted in a much more buoyant establishment after 1850. By the 1890s, many of the most successful forms of leisure and sociability were Anglican innovations (although some of the most famous, such as Everton and Aston Villa football clubs, were ventures of Victorian Methodists). Church of England Sunday Schools reached a phenomenal proportion of the population and continued to grow into the twentieth century. However, the confrontation with the many challenges explored in this chapter left the Church divided along multiple faultlines. One of these was a split between Low, High, and Broad Church.

These terms indicate three different visions of the Church's future. In making sense of the distinctions between them, it is crucial to recognize that there is a sliding scale between Protestant and Catholic: these are not really opposed, mutually exclusive categories, but two ends of a continuous spectrum of possible approaches to Christianity in the Western tradition.

The Church of England saw itself as practising a 'middle way'. Anglicans distrusted the Roman Catholic Church, which they saw as demanding blind obedience to a plutocratic Pope; however, they also distrusted 'extreme' Protestantism, associated with Germanic sects, which they felt possessed no respect for authority. Many Protestant sects, including Methodism, placed a strong emphasis on individualism. In its formal hierarchical structure, the Church of England resembled Catholicism. In its emphasis on personal immersion in scripture, it was Protestant. The terms High, Low, and Broad denote different attitudes to Catholic and Protestant elements within the Church.

The term Low Church indicates those parts of the Church of England with the closest affinities to evangelicalism. Evangelical Anglicans were the most emphatically Protestant element of the Church and their growth and predominance was the most notable feature of early Victorian Anglicanism. Their worship was simple. It rejected rituals involving incense or elaborate vestments. But this did not mean it was quiet or austere. In this period, evangelical Anglicans fostered links with flamboyant American evangelists such as Dwight Moody and Ira Sankey who toured England in the 1870s; over the next fifty years, a staggering 80 million copies of Sankey's hymnbook *Sacred Songs and Solos* were printed in Britain. Low Church services were full of song and emotional rhetoric. Sermons, which in the hands of some evangelical preachers could last hours, sometimes spoke of the horrors of hell and the ecstasy of salvation but were sometimes much more homely and reassuring, promising 'entire sanctification'. This was the part of the Church that aimed to save souls around the world by raising money for missions to convert the 'heathen'. Evangelicalism, however, could be full of optimism as well as stark warnings of damned souls. This unpretentious hope for a transformed future is conveyed in a hymn by the evangelical preacher (and later leader of a Methodist sect) Hugh Bourne:

The Lord a glorious work begun
And thro' America it run,
Across the sea it flies;
This work is now to us come near,
And many are converted here,
We see it with our eyes.

In contrast, the High Church was where a well-known Victorian description of the Church of England – 'the Tory Party at prayer' – rang most true. High Churchmen were typically of more elevated social status than their Low Church peers. They practised a more formal and elaborate ritual and displayed less overt emotion. The most significant story of the mid-Victorian Church is the resurgence of High Church Anglicanism. Reacting against evangelicalism, some elements in the High Church began to move closer to Catholicism. In the hands of these groups, known variously as Anglo-Catholics, ritualists, tractarians, or the Oxford Movement, churchmen reminded their contemporaries that sixteenth-century reformers had created Anglicanism as 'the one true Catholic Church' in England.

The Anglo-Catholic outgrowth from the High Church was fiercely contested. Its practitioners, such as E.B. Pusey and J.H. Newman, were among the most controversial public figures in Victorian Britain. This controversy increased as several leading Anglo-Catholics made high-profile conversions to Roman Catholicism. Converts included members of leading Church of England families, such as the Wilberforces (Robert), Bensons (Robert Hugh), and of course the Newmans (John Henry). It is difficult now to recover the shock and anguish caused by these conversions. Leading statesmen such as Gladstone wept when their friends 'turned to Rome'. Catholic converts were often disowned and despised by friends and family.

THE CATHOLIC REVIVAL

The Roman Catholic Church is the largest body of Christians in the world, but it did not play a particularly prominent role in early nineteenth-century England, Wales, or Scotland. This slowly changed. In 1829, Catholics were given full civil rights, including the right to be elected as MPs. In 1840, Parliament recognized the authority of Catholicism in Ireland by ending support for the Anglican Church as the official Church of Ireland.

The most prominent Catholic in mid-Victorian Britain was John Henry Newman. Newman had been a leading light of the Church of England until his conversion in 1845. He helped establish a Catholic university in Ireland, which was the occasion of one of his most important publications: *The Idea of a University* (1852). His *Apologia Pro Vita Sua* (1864) is the century's classic work of spiritual autobiography. Newman was a controversial but much loved figure whose conversion was seen to represent a crisis of Anglicanism. It occurred at the same time as the most dramatic events in Victorian Catholicism, when Pope Pius IX reinstated the Roman Catholic Church structure in Britain, appointing an unpopular figure, Nicholas Wiseman, as Catholic Archbishop of Westminster in 1850.

Numbers of Catholics in England, Wales, and Scotland increased over the following decades. By 1900, Catholicism was treated with much less fear and hostility. One mark of this is that the most significant musical work of Victorian Britain was a setting by a Catholic composer, Edward Elgar, of Newman's Catholic poem *The Dream of Gerontius* (1900). This was performed in Anglican settings including Worcester Cathedral and was celebrated as a triumph of English music.

By mid-century, there was a host of deep antagonisms within the Church and between churchmen and dissenters. The 1851 census revealed an image of national religious beliefs that churchmen found deeply shocking. This was the first (and only) census to ask Britons about their churchgoing. It showed that a surprisingly small proportion had attended a Church of England service on 'census Sunday'. Only around half the population had been to a service at all, and of these half had been part of dissenting congregations. Until 1851, Anglicanism had often seemed synonymous with Englishness: many clergymen assumed that the Church represented the nation in a straightforward way. The blunt statistics of the census ended this complacency.

The mission of the Broad Church was to soothe institutional antagonisms and to recreate a situation in which the Church of England was a national, representative entity. Broad Churchmen, also known as liberal Anglicans, argued that Church of England dogma should be relaxed and demand for strict conformity to the thirty-nine articles abandoned. In this way, they hoped, Methodists and other dissenters could be 'returned to the fold'. Broad Churchmen such as A.P. Stanley, Dean of Westminster, agonized over the relationships between Christianity and new developments in historical and scientific knowledge, which seemed to make traditional readings of scripture unsustainable. Reconciling science and religion was as much a Broad Church project as reconciling Anglicans and Methodists.

In the mid-Victorian years, the Broad Church was just one among many efforts to re-unify British Protestants. The Free Christian Union, founded in 1867, was created by the most liberal and undogmatic of all Victorian dissenting groups, the Unitarians. The Union's agenda was to offer a common meeting place for Protestants of all descriptions, demanding no particulars of dogma. Christian morality, they insisted, was more important than the details of specific Christian beliefs. Debates within this movement tested the boundaries of acceptable Christian opinion. Did Christians have to believe that Christ was the son of God? The Free Christian Union answered that they did not. After three years, the Union collapsed, in part because its members could not agree on where Christianity ended and other religions began. Some commentators, including J.H. Newman's brother, Francis, called for 'union between all theists': a religious union must permit access to those who had rejected Christ's authority including Jews, Muslims, and Hindus. When the Hindu thinker Keshab Chandra Sen toured British Christian institutions in 1870, calls for a general Theistic Catholic Church were conceived as a step towards 'the future Church of the world'. These calls were never answered, but Britain was slowly becoming more diverse and more aware of difference: the question of how to deal with religious variety exercised many different people.

Challenges to tradition: liberal theology and scientific naturalism

Religious transformations of many kinds took place across the Victorian period. Explanations for why this happened usually take one of three forms. Some are written from the perspective of the Church: they use the decisions made by church leaders to explain change. These 'supply side' accounts ask whether or not the strategies chosen by church institutions worked: could the Church 'keep up' with change? Others are social histories that explore how urbanization and industrialization brought people into new forms of social organization and therefore changed their behaviour. These tend to use church attendance to measure religious convictions in different regions.

The third kind of history narrates changes in the intellectual environment within which churches and believers operated. If the Bible had been the primary guide to life for early Victorians, it was rivalled by a host of competing modes of thought later in the century. Charles Darwin has long been used to symbolize a supposed assault of science against religion. However, to think of this as an 'attack' or to imagine that there were two broad entities – 'science' and 'religion' – that could be pitched against each other is to misunderstand a world in which most scientific thinkers were deeply religious, and most challenges to traditional interpretations of the Bible actually came from within religious thought.

The rise of liberal theology is a crucial aspect of Victorian religious change. The main events occurred in the German states among Protestant intellectuals who endeavoured to modernize and revitalize Christianity by stripping it of what they saw as mythology and superstition. Some elements in the Bible, they insisted, were incompatible with progressive, rational thought: these were products of overactive human imaginations and should therefore be weeded out. What remained would be a purified body of religious truth.

This biblical criticism began by questioning the mythic narratives of the Old Testament, such as the flood of Noah. However, its most profound impact came through assertions that New Testament miracles, including Christ's resurrection, were not records of real events but the products of the 'mythically excited imaginations' of early Christians. For a critic such as Ernst Renan, Jesus had been purely human. The Gospels were the biography of an exemplary teacher whose teachings should be followed but who was not the son of God.

These ideas took a long time to filter through British society. They were championed by George Eliot, among others, in the 1840s; several churchmen controversially supported them in the 1860s; only after 1870, however, did they arouse widespread interest among the reading public. One of the most powerful forces in popularizing these ideas was a novel entitled *Robert Elsmere* (1886) by Mary Augusta Ward. The novel's title character is a student at Oxford on track to become an Anglican clergyman. However, he undertakes research on medieval French history, which transforms his religious outlook. He is horrified to find that he can no longer read the Gospels as historical texts: 'his trained historical sense, the keen instrument he had sharpened so laboriously on indifferent material now ploughed its agonising way, bit by bit into the most intimate recesses of his thought and faith'.

Significantly, Elsmere continues to believe in God and to be a kind of Christian. Yet he cannot adhere to the teachings of the Church or to belief in Christ as divine. He follows the example of Jesus in committing his life to aiding the London poor and attempts to encourage a new form of religion without dogma or creeds. Elsmere's definition of religion is that described by Matthew Arnold (Ward's famous uncle) in *Literature and Dogma* (1873): 'morality touched by emotion'. This is not a definition that could have been written any time before the late nineteenth century.

Working in parallel to liberal theology, although initially less dramatic in their impact, were new approaches to the sciences. At the beginning of the Victorian period, few people thought of 'science' and 'religion' as things that could ever be in competition. The term 'scientist' was coined in 1834 by William Whewell, a Cambridge mathematician. Like most writers on science, Whewell was a Church of England clergyman. 'Clergyman' and 'scientist' were in fact two pursuits that fitted very neatly together for early Victorians. The most prominent approach to scientific thought was known as natural theology. It treated nature (God's works) as a record of the mind of the creator: studying the natural sciences was therefore as much an act of Christian devotion as reading the Bible (God's word).

Natural theology slowly lost prestige in the early Victorian years. Professionalization in many fields followed hot on the heels of industrialization and encouraged the increasing separation of different forms of expertise. This was a key moment in discipline formation. Universities slowly began to teach disciplines beyond the established trio of classics, theology, and mathematics. This made it necessary to decide precisely where the task of one scholar (for example, the biologist) ended and that of another (e.g. the chemist) began.

The idea that theology and the natural sciences were separate was new and significant. It did not change the fact that most scientific thinkers were deeply religious individuals, but it did make it easier for 'scientists' to think and act outside frameworks established by the Church.

After mid-century, a new class of professional scientists fought hard to ensure the independence of their discipline. Natural theology was abandoned as a philosophy of science, and professionalizers such as T.H. Huxley sought to replace it with a strident new vision. This was known as scientific naturalism. It insisted that only those things that can be measured or tested are real: the scientific thinker should remain neutral on all questions that cannot be answered by experiment or observation.

Huxley and his peers fought a vigorous campaign to make certain that knowledge created in the new sciences would not be accepted or rejected only in so far as it accorded with custom, prejudice, or religious tradition. They aimed to establish a 'scientocracy' in which scientists would replace the clergy as the first port of call for people with questions concerning life, the universe, and everything. Some scientific naturalists adopted a philosophy of materialism. This insisted that the human mind is a product of the material structure of the brain and that the brain itself was a product of unguided evolution.

The relationship between new scientific knowledge and religious tradition was handled differently by almost every commentator in Victorian Britain. Debates on scientific thought among clergyman were often subject to more public controversy than statements of scientists themselves. The most famous such controversy began when seven leading clergymen published a collection of *Essays and Reviews* (1860), which called on the Church of England to embrace both liberal theology and the discoveries of scientific naturalists. One essay, by George Baden Powell (father of the founder of the scouting movement), presented God as creator of scientific laws. It insisted, as had the German critics, that the idea of biblical miracles was not religion but superstition. Another, by Benjamin Jowett, argued that the Bible should be read as a product of its time. It should not be expected to have anything to say concerning subsequent advances in scientific knowledge.

The Church hierarchy attacked *Essays and Reviews* as heretical, subjecting two of its contributors to long and shambolic trials in a church court. Conservative commentators labelled them 'the seven against Christ' and published a multitude of counter-arguments. However, this bestselling volume had already shown the public that an extraordinary range of opinion existed in the highest echelons of the Church as to the relationships between Anglican tradition, liberal theology, and scientific naturalism. In the following decade, many clergymen fitted evolutionary thought into their worldviews, while others rejected it. By the 1880s, the opinions expressed in *Essays and Reviews* could be espoused much more easily: they were no longer heretical but part of the very wide spectrum of respectable beliefs.

Comparison and diversity: looking beyond the Church

In 1882, a writer from a prominent Victorian family, William Simcox, wrote the following in a major periodical, *The Academy*:

> There is probably still a majority of educated Englishmen who believe as heartily as they believed five-and-twenty years ago … in the truth of the Bible. Still, before 1860, they not only believed in these doctrines, but thought that the world was agreed on them, that all who doubted them were actuated … at best by a habit of paradoxical reasoning that had destroyed their common sense. But between 1860 and 1870 they learnt that … their belief was rejected by men who were virtuous, candid, and intelligent; between 1870 and 1882 they have learnt that virtuous, candid, and intelligent men may be not only unorthodox or rationalistic thinkers, but in the common sense of the words, atheists and materialists.

This was a perceptive summary of what had occurred. In the same period, the British had also learned a great deal about other religions and had become considerably more receptive to the insights these religions could offer.

In the 1850s, the Jewish Lord Mayor of London, David Salomons, had campaigned vigorously for full political rights for Jews. This was achieved in 1858 and Baron Lionel de Rothschild became the first Jewish MP in the same year. In 1868, Benjamin Disraeli, from a Jewish family, became Prime Minister.

The first atheist MP was far more controversial. Charles Bradlaugh was elected in 1880, but forcibly removed from the House of Commons and denied his seat because he refused to swear allegiance to God. Only after being re-elected four times did he take his seat in 1886.

Most early Victorians had not even recognized Islam as a religion (considering it a perversion of Christianity). Thomas Carlyle's treatment of Muhammad in an 1840 lecture, 'The Hero as Prophet', caused great consternation because of its admiring tone (although that is not how it reads today). By 1869, there was a Muslim convert, Henry Stanley, sitting in the House of Lords and lobbying in the interests of Muslims in the empire. In 1887, another Muslim convert, William Quilliam, began a conversionary mission in Liverpool. He established a British Muslim Association and Liverpool Muslim Institute, undertook extensive philanthropic work, and converted at least five hundred Britons. During the 1890s, Quilliam was a prominent Imam in a multicultural British city who was sent gifts including a stallion by the Caliph of Sunni Islam.

Several bestsellers, such as Edwin Arnold's poetic life of Buddha *The Light of Asia: The Great Renunciation* (1879), encouraged late Victorians to think deeply about religions other than their own. In the year that Arnold's work was issued, Friedrich Max Müller began publishing a major scholarly project, *The Sacred Books of the East*. By 1910, this series ran to fifty volumes, including documents of Islam, Buddhism, Hinduism, Taoism, Confucianism, Jainism, and Zoroastrianism.

By the close of the Victorian period, Britain was home to a phenomenal range of age-old religious traditions but British towns and cities also saw new spiritual innovations. Among the most novel were the spiritualists who made it their business to communicate with the dead. The fragility of life in the Victorian city meant that every Briton was acquainted with death, and large numbers turned to séances and other forms of spiritualist communication to try to make sense of loss. Like evangelicalism, spiritualism was a transatlantic movement, emerging in 1840s America and spreading through Britain by letter writing and networks of travelling enthusiasts. Most spiritualists considered their practices to be unproblematically Christian, directly related to events in the New Testament and ideas such as 'the communion of Saints'. This allowed leading churchmen and statesmen, including William Gladstone, to exercise an interest in the movement. No phenomenon better illustrates the inseparability of Victorian scientific and religious thought than the Society for Psychical Research, founded in 1882 by several leading Victorian thinkers to use scientific methods to analyse the truths and falsities of spiritualist claims to communicate with the realms of the dead.

Going a step further than spiritualists, late Victorian occultists practised ritual magic within intricate formal hierarchies. They created an alternative rationality in protest against the 'instrumental reason' of scientific rationalism. To build their rituals, they drew on Indian, Egyptian, Graeco-Roman, and Celtic traditions, although (as with spiritualists) the vast majority retained affiliation to Christian denominations. In *The Place of Enchantment: British Occultism and the Culture of the Modern* (2004), Alex Owen produced a scintillating study of this tradition, making it a case study of the roles of reason and imagination in modernity. Despite its apparently niche subject matter, this book is unrivalled as an intricate, sophisticated portrait of late Victorian culture and ideas.

Diversity was exhilarating to many Victorians, but to others it suggested that the fabric of society was unravelling. The Church had responded to the spiritual free market with an extravagant wave of church building. However, church authorities took other measures too. These involved expanding the Church's provision far beyond the simple Sunday service. The phenomenon whereby the Church became involved in leisure and social life has been labelled 'diffusive Christianity'.

Among the most dramatic 'diffusive' roles the Church took on was that of focal point for major public events. Buildings such as St Paul's Cathedral and Westminster Abbey became sites of national memory and mourning. Huge funerals of public figures could sell over 10,000 tickets. Among the first of these enormous funerals was that of Wellington in 1852: it is estimated that more than 5% of the total British population saw his funeral cortege pass. The Church quickly became an inclusive 'national Valhalla', not just a place for Anglican dignitaries to be interred. A.P. Stanley, Dean of Westminster Abbey from 1864 to 1881, oversaw lavish funerals for public figures who were not respectable Anglicans, including Charles Dickens, Palmerston, and the explorer David Livingston. The sermons of celebrity churchmen such as Henry Parry Liddon and Henry Drummond were printed in newspapers and could sell over a million copies in pamphlets: they were among the most prominent public figures at the century's close. Churchmen could enjoy greater celebrity, although much less official authority, than they had in 1837.

These developments showed that the role of the Church of England had changed. It was not now a powerful, authoritarian arm of the state itself, but a public guide on questions of morality and an orchestrator of local and national events. It had invented for itself a strong cultural role within a rich and multifarious free market in religion.

7

Reforming class: politics and the social order

The belly, the brain and the bone of modern society.

This phrase was a late Victorian cliché used, for example, by the President of the Birmingham and Edgbaston Debating Society in 1892. It was intended to indicate three distinct parts of the British social order. The aristocracy – 'the belly' – was notable for its taste and appetite; the middle-class 'brain' was made up of managers, professionals, and bureaucrats; and working-class graft was the skeleton that sustained the social structure. The debating society president used this phrase during the heyday of social divisions by economic class. Trade Unionism and socialist politics were growing and the Labour Party would be formed as a parliamentary pressure group just a few years later. 1890s Britain seemed to be a society divided cleanly into three.

Social divisions were certainly not illusory. Victorian Britain was an intensely unequal society. An upper-class commodity such as a box at the Royal Opera House typically cost more than the lifetime wages for a domestic servant. The gulfs between the labouring poor and the moderately well-off were greater even than in Britain today, making social mobility difficult and meaning that the streets and homes in which Victorian labourers lived looked and felt entirely different from those populated by the middle classes. This is one reason why 'telling the story' of this period is so complex: for several decades, the lot of the well-off improved, and progress was therefore celebrated, while the deprivation confronted by the poor only intensified.

'Class' is the idea that has been most widely used to make sense of inequality. Yet it is only one option among many for exploring the social structure. Class analysis usually implies the division of society into three tiers derived from economic function. The working, middle, and upper classes map directly onto labour, capital (the resources associated with factories, mills, and trade), and landed wealth. It is usually assumed that from these economic facts inferences can be drawn concerning culture, identity, and political commitments.

Although class was developed into an intensely sophisticated tool by Marxist historians of the mid-twentieth century, in most usages it is a blunt instrument. Victorian society was complex, and became increasingly intricate as new occupations proliferated: to divide the diverse citizens of so complex a society into three tiers is self-evidently an enormously broad-brush act. It can only drive analysis if we know for certain that those citizens understood their own place in the social order in terms of these same class distinctions. Class consciousness (class as a cultural idea) thus becomes as significant as the blunt facts of an individual's place in a spectrum of earnings or occupation (class as economic fact).

The historiography of class

Since the mid-twentieth century, there have been many ways of relating the concept of class to the Victorian social structure. The most influential is found in E.P. Thompson's *Making of the English Working Class* (1963). This book's preface is often among the first things students of the nineteenth century read. It is an impassioned advocacy of the power of one particular vision of class to recover the lives of the disempowered in the early nineteenth century.

After losing his youthful faith in communism in the 1950s, Thompson developed a version of socialist history formed around the principle of 'history from below'. This phrase does not simply mean studying the disempowered in society, but studying society from the perspective of the disempowered. It denotes the techniques involved in recovering the worldviews of past people, rather than simply the act of studying the poor.

To Thompson, the fundamental dynamic of modern history was the reorganization of society into the three tiers of class. However, he insisted that class was not a 'structure', a 'category', or a 'thing'. It was neither a static entity nor an abstract principle. In insisting that class was a dynamic relationship between specific people, Thompson felt that he could restore dignity to the workers of the past: class, he insisted, is defined by people 'as they live their own history, and, in the end, this is its only definition'. Class was therefore something that happened

> When some men, as a result of common experiences (inherited or shared), feel and articulate the identity of interests as between themselves, and as against other men whose interests are different from (and usually opposed to) theirs. The class experience is largely determined by the productive relations into which men are born – or enter involuntarily. Class-consciousness is the way in which these experiences are handled in cultural terms: embodied in traditions, value systems, ideas and institutional forms. If the experience appears as determined, class-consciousness does not.

In this way, Thompson insisted that class formation was an active process that labourers achieved for themselves.

The most widely quoted of all Thompson's famous statements reveals the powerful humane agenda behind his work:

> I am seeking to rescue the poor stockinger, the Luddite cropper, the 'obsolete' hand-loom weaver, the 'utopian' artisan, and even the deluded follower of Joanna Southcott, from the enormous condescension of posterity. Their crafts and traditions may have been dying. Their hostility to the new industrialism may have been backward-looking. Their communitarian ideals may have been fantasies. Their insurrectionary conspiracies may have been foolhardy. But they lived through these times of acute social disturbance, and we did not. Their aspirations were valid in terms of their own experience; and, if they were casualties of history, they remain, condemned in their own lives, as casualties.

Thompson's chronology sees the working class as substantially 'made' by the beginning of the Victorian period. By this point, he argues, regional divisions had faded and 'the working-class presence was ... the most significant actor in British political life'. In Thompson's view, society in 1837 was already structured and understood in terms of its 'belly', 'brain', and 'bones'; the pre-industrial age when society was split between an active aristocracy and passive plebs had ended.

Historians have challenged Thompson's vision of class on several grounds, ranging from his blunt dismissal of more orthodox Marxist approaches to, more significantly, the almost total absence of women from his vision. Others, such as the social historian Keith Snell, have insisted that the continued localism of Victorian life discouraged the emergence of national fellow-feeling among labouring people and delayed the consolidation of a working class until the middle of the century. As the historian of politics and religion Boyd Hilton argues, 'class was experienced one way in a town like Birmingham, with its small, family-run workshops, and quite differently in Manchester, with its huge factories and stark opposition between masters and men'.

David Cannadine insists that Thompson's portrait of the early nineteenth century is a simple misdiagnosis: neither a working class nor a middle class was 'made' in this period. In fact, Cannadine claims, the actual fabric of society barely changed. 'What *was* going on was an unprecedentedly agitated discussion of social structure, which ebbed and flowed, as contemporaries could not agree – and did not want to agree' as to how their society should be interpreted. The options they failed to choose between included, firstly, an almost feudal spectrum of hierarchical statuses, or, secondly, a three-class structure in which a 'middle' mediated between the poor and those in power. At least as influential as either of these was a third option: a stark binary in which aristocracy, government, the Church, law, the East India Company, and the banks wielded power and everyone else ('the people') was subject to their will.

The most interesting challenge to the predominance of class has come from Patrick Joyce. Joyce is editor of the leading handbook *Class*. In his own research, he has urged historians not to assume the presence of class ideas or class language, but to analyse the roles of class and its alternatives afresh for every case study they tackle. Class, in Joyce's view, should not be a master narrative when we describe the Victorian social structure, but one small aspect of a complex story. This is how he begins *Democratic Subjects*, his study of two nineteenth-century men, Edwin Waugh and John Bright:

> This history is the story of two men, and of the stories they and others told in order that it might be known who they were. It is a history of identity, about 'the self' and about 'the social', the latter in the sense of collective identities, and the contexts in which these are set. The quotation marks signal that these terms have significance

> in so far as their meanings are made by us, and not found … in a world beyond this assignment of meaning. In thinking about identities in the past, whether of the 'self' or of the collective, class has, until recently, occupied a very considerable role among social historians … The sorrows of Edwin Waugh and the measured certainties of John Bright, serve to question this dominance, as do the democratic romances that gave shape to the social and political imagination of millions of their contemporaries. Other forms of the self and of collective identity emerge, long obscured by the concentration on class. And class itself, like any other 'social' subject, is seen to be an imagined form, not something given in a 'real' world.

Whatever we make of Joyce's assault on class, or the less dramatic critiques of Cannadine and Snell, it is clear that the status of class as the fundamental social dynamic of modern history can no longer be taken for granted.

As a tool of social commentary and self-explanation for the Victorians themselves, class ebbed and flowed across the period. The purpose of this chapter will be to explore the process whereby class, by the end of the century, did become a primary lens through which Victorians made sense of themselves. Along the way, it will investigate those moments, particularly the 1840s, when class helped make sense of social change; and those moments, such as the 1850s and 60s, when other ways of interpreting society were preferred.

Reform and the 'middle classes' in the 1830s

Many historians, including Thompson, have insisted that before the late eighteenth century the 'middle class' was not a distinctive, visible presence. The political life of the nation operated in terms of a binary between a patrician elite and plebeian society. Some historians use the term 'middling sorts' to describe those who occupied the middle ground – neither powerful nor poor – in that polarized society.

There is a traditional explanation for how this situation changed. It suggests that the decline of the landed aristocracy, and the rise of a middle class, was the product of industrial revolution. As industry expanded, capital replaced land and property as the dominant part of the economy. This new wealth persuaded politicians to recognize the middle class as a political player: in 1832, the Great Reform Act enfranchised the middle classes and ended the era when Parliament was a plaything for the landed elite.

This story is too simple. The industrial revolution was slower and patchier than was once thought; consequently, those who benefited from it were more diverse than this image suggests. Aristocratic power continued to control much of British society. Even at the height of Britain's status as a nation of factories (which arrived, anyway, after 1900), manufacturing interests were always dwarfed by land, property, and finance.

The relationship between the middle classes and the reforms of 1832 is also equivocal. The politician who introduced the key reform bill, Lord Russell, did not mention the middle classes when he presented the bill to Parliament: empowering a middle class does not seem to have been his priority. Only later, as the bill was debated, did a backbench MP (the historian T.B. Macaulay) make a rousing speech that framed reform as the struggle of the 'middle classes in England' against an arbitrary aristocracy. Macaulay's interjection changed the tone of debate. Next day, Lord Palmerston, an up-and-coming Whig, spoke in favour of that middle class 'distinguished by morality and good conduct – by obedience to the laws … by attachment to the Throne'. Robert Peel retorted that these middling sorts were a 'vulgar privileged pedlary … the class just above physical force, which has no quality attracting respect'.

Another MP, Horace Twiss, noted their 'narrow minds and bigoted views': the involvement of the middle classes in politics, he insisted, would end rational government.

In this way, the Reform Act of 1832 did put the middle class at the centre of debate, but it did not represent their triumph. In fact, reform was so protective of aristocratic hierarchies that the leading Whig, Lord Grey, labelled it 'the most aristocratic measure that ever was proposed in Parliament'.

In the light of all these challenges, historians have largely abandoned the question of when a middle class came to exist and instead ask questions concerning the *idea* of a middle class. In *Imagining the Middle Class* (1995), Dror Wahrman explores 'how, why and when … the British came to believe that they lived in a society centred around a "middle class"'. Other recent studies of the middle class, such as Franco Moretti's *The Bourgeois* (2013), also analyse ways in which 'the middle' has been conceptualized rather than writing the history of a specific, describable class.

However, the Reform Act of 1832 is still often seen as the moment at which the idea of a large, respectable, and productive middle class took centre stage in social thought. Cosy middle-class domesticity continues to play a large role in most visions of the Victorians, and this period is often labelled 'the bourgeois age'. Two more pieces of legislation that favoured the middle classes followed closely on the heels of reform. The Municipal Corporations Act (1835) gave new autonomy to city councils, allowing the wealthier commercial classes greater control of cities such as Manchester and Birmingham: cities, some argued, were being handed from aristocrats to the middle classes. The repeal of the Corn Laws (1846) was praised as a middle-class victory, marking a transition of power from landed interests (who wished to maintain the high price of corn) to the commercial classes (who were committed to the ideal of a free market without artificial controls).

The middle class could still not be measured statistically by occupation, income, or anything else, but the worldviews of professionals, commerce, and well-to-do moralizers were beginning to be seen as distinctively middle-class visions. They have been analysed since as the middle-class ideology that shaped the emergence of Victorian culture. This ideology reached its height in the 1850s and 60s (explored below) but there is no doubt that the 1830s were a key moment in its formulation.

The working classes in the 1840s

Lagging slightly behind the idea of a unified middle was the idea of a working class. The political activism of 'the hungry forties', particularly Chartism, was instrumental in making the working class visible to the authorities, but also to themselves. Sometimes described as the first national working-class movement in British history, Chartism was celebrated at the time as an unprecedented flexing of working-class muscle.

The People's Charter, a demand for democratic representation after which the Chartist movement was named, was drafted in 1838. Written in London, it was launched in Glasgow at a meeting attended by 150,000 people. Presented to Parliament by the (middle-class) Birmingham banker Thomas Attwood, the Charter carried a staggering 1,280,958 signatures. Nevertheless, Parliament voted to dismiss it without consideration. The next decade was characterized by continued campaigning to address, as the *Bradford Herald* put it, 'the social wants and hopes of the working classes'.

Behind the rallying cry of the People's Charter, Chartists fought to create a politics of class. Chartist papers and pamphlets drew attention to deep divides between those who owned resources and those whose only resource was their labour. They aimed to weaken the grip of 'deference'. This term denotes the 'bonds of attachment' that defined relationships between those of different statuses, dictating the intense respect that an agricultural hand should show to a clergyman or a clergyman to the local lord. Writing in the wake of the first French Revolution, Edmund Burke, outspoken critic of democracy, had called deference the 'generous loyalty to rank' possessed by British people above all others. Chartist politics implied a switch from 'vertical' loyalties between worker, employer, and landowner to 'horizontal' loyalties between all those labourers who were dispossessed of the products of their work by the command of idle authorities.

Several regions of Britain proved particularly central to the class agitations of the 1840s. These included the Celtic nations, where class antagonisms were exacerbated by nationalist politics. Newport in South Wales saw the most intense violence of the Chartist movement, when Nonconformist Welsh labourers marched on the town centre, protesting against Anglican middle-class power. Chartism was also powerful in Glasgow, where the gulf in conditions between the comfortable and the poor was such that life expectancy for labourers was less than half that of their employers.

THE PEOPLE'S CHARTER

The front page of the charter indicated the nature of its demands, including its six key points. It read in full:

The People's Charter; being the outline of an act to provide for the just representation of the people of Great Britain in the Commons' House of Parliament:

Embracing the principles of
Universal Suffrage
No Property Qualification
Annual Parliaments
Equal Representation
Payment of Members
and Vote by Ballot

> *Prepared by a Committee of Twelve Persons, six members of Parliament and six members of the London Working Men's Association, and addressed to the people of the United Kingdom.*
>
> The Charter's headline was the demand that all men over the age of 21 should receive the vote (even by 1838 only 18% of adult males could vote). It also proposed the redistribution of parliamentary seats: the United Kingdom would be divided into 300 districts, each with the same number of voters. In this way, every vote would carry equal weight in returning members of Parliament. The demand for payment of MPs was intended to ensure that those who were not independently wealthy might stand.

Most horrifically, the clash between English leaders and impoverished people claimed a million lives in Ireland in the late 1840s. The Irish potato famines began in a series of natural disasters, with blight destroying crops. By 1847, the situation could have been under control: enough grain was imported to Ireland to feed the population. However, the distribution of food was so unequal – so divided along class and political lines – that the famine intensified. In deliberate efforts to encourage 'self-reliance' and 'self-exertion', agricultural labourers were permitted little in the way of assistance and thrown back on their own inadequate resources. In 1848, the politician responsible for poor relief in Ireland, Sir Charles Trevelyan, published his interpretation of the crisis. He explained that the deaths associated with the famine were rooted in the immoral nature of the Irish rather than in economic factors. He insisted that God had sent the famine as a 'sharp but effectual remedy' to the failings of the Irish agrarian system: starving Irish peasants, in Trevelyan's view, were getting their just deserts. Nowhere was the 'us' against 'them' antagonism of the 1840s more evident.

If Ireland saw the most intense horrors of the hungry forties, Manchester embodied the politics of Chartism itself. The city was so exemplary and extreme that it drew a multitude of observers, most famously Marx and Engels, to examine its conditions. They travelled to Manchester to publicize the horrific conditions of the poor. But they also wished to reveal the possibilities hidden within this human tragedy. This was, in their view, a galvanizing horror, which would result in the rise of the oppressed labouring classes into the most powerful political force ever seen. It was precisely because Manchester was capitalism's most intense horror that it was also the greatest hope for the future. 'Manchester', wrote Engels, 'is the seat of the most powerful Unions, the central point of Chartism, the place which numbers the most socialists'.

Paul Pickering's *Chartism and the Chartists in Manchester and Salford* (1995) conjures the world through which Chartist protesters marched on numerous occasions in the 1840s. Pickering shows how the organization of the city gave birth to an intense class politics. Chartist marches began from the city's commercial hub where most establishments were closed to labourers. The glittering drapers of Market Street, with crystal chandeliers, stood close to the Royal Exchange, built in 1809, where the manufacturing elite, the 'Parliament of Cotton Lords', presided over the city's economic fate. A host of ugly warehouses and drab factories engulfed this small presentable enclave: these 'hissing, whizzing, jumping, thumping, rattling, steaming and stinking' factories were noted by one marcher as 'the bitterest curse' of the poor.

Next, Chartist marchers reached regions that were more familiar, but no more welcoming. The Manchester Workhouse, or 'poor law Bastille', loomed over a sea of slums. The neighbouring Paupers' Burial Ground housed tens of thousands of unmarked graves reminding the poor that even in death they were inferior. These working-class districts were crammed around the Rivers Irwell and Irk, national symbols of industry's potential to degrade nature. Thousands lived here in damp cellars that were frequently flooded by the filthy rivers.

THE WORKHOUSE

Before 1834, British parishes had distributed substantial amounts of money in poor relief. However, this relatively generous system had become incompatible with laissez-faire economics. The New Poor Law of 1834 insisted that 'all relief whatever to able-bodied persons or to their families, otherwise than in well-regulated workhouses (i.e. places where they may be set to work…) shall be declared unlawful'. This is not quite what happened (poor relief continued to be administered at about two-thirds its previous level) but workhouses did play a much larger practical and symbolic role in Victorian society than they ever had before.

The workhouse system was calculated to be stern and forbidding. The architecture of its buildings was often calculated to tower over poor areas as a threat. The system separated families, including mothers and young children. It enforced rigid discipline and crippling levels of physical toil. In 1841, G.R. Wythen Baxter published a famous work, *The Book of the Bastiles*, which compiled hundreds of reports on the inhumanity of workhouses. Descriptions of the brutal beating of young children, often for the most innocuous of misdemeanours, caused particularly vocal outcries. Later in the 1840s, a series of scandals demonized the workhouse still further. In Andover in 1845, inmates who were commanded to 'crush bones' were reported to be so starved that they scavenged the tiniest flecks of decayed meat. In 1848, the Huddersfield workhouse was reported to be so cramped that it packed children ten to the bed, corpses were left sharing beds with the living, and the sick were untended to.

Unsurprisingly workhouses, including that in Stockport near Manchester, became targets for demonstrators and rioters. The system survived, however, beyond the end of the Victorian period.

Among the most striking features of these deprived districts was the success with which they were hidden from the main arteries of travel through the city. Manchester's working class, according to the Irish journalist and campaigner William Cooke-Taylor in 1844,

> live, hidden from the view of the higher ranks by piles of stores, mills, warehouses, and manufacturing

> establishments, less known to their wealthy neighbours … than the inhabitants of New Zealand.

In no city was the separation of rich and poor starker than in Manchester. In no region did Chartism more closely approximate to the war of a unified working class against moneyed interests. By 1840, it was rumoured that Manchester Chartists had acquired five brass cannons. They were said to be running a brisk trade in gunpowder and compiling an armoury of handarms with which to wage class war. Here, if anywhere, class politics was more than a niche pursuit and class interests defined the outlook of large numbers of people.

There is, however, no more pivotal moment in the dramatic narrative of Manchester's burgeoning class antagonism than its sudden collapse. 1850s Manchester was a surprisingly bourgeois and peaceable place. In 1857, the city hosted an exhibition entitled Art Treasures of Great Britain. With 16,000 works of art and 1.3 million visitors, Britain has never seen an exhibition of the fine arts more expansive and ambitious than this. That Manchester was its chosen site attested to class harmony and a bourgeois self-assurance unthreatened by class divisions. How had this happened?

A profound caesura?

It will hardly be surprising that class tensions have been most evident in tense times, but the scale of the change between the strife-torn 1840s and the prosperous 1850s is unexpectedly dramatic. After 1848, class divisions did not cost politicians much sleep, nor were numerous workers willing to risk their lives in pursuit of class politics. This period has been labelled an 'economic golden age', the 'age of equipoise', and 'the great mid-Victorian social peace'. All such labels imply that the 1850s and 60s saw 'a profound caesura' in the battle of class against class.

THE GREAT EXHIBITION OF THE WORKS OF INDUSTRY OF ALL NATIONS

- This exhibition was held in a vast, purpose-built structure of glass and iron – the Crystal Palace – erected in Hyde Park in 1851. Organized by a Royal Society for the Encouragement of Arts, Manufactures and Commerce, the exhibition was championed by Prince Albert.
- 1,851 ft long and 454 ft wide, the plate-glass and cast-iron frame was designed by Joseph Paxton and manufactured in Birmingham and Smethwick. Inside, trees and large statues emphasized the scale of the structure. 13,000 exhibits from Britain, its 'colonies and dependencies', and 44 'foreign nations' were displayed. These ranged from art and stained glass to scientific instruments, industrial technologies (including a whole, working cotton mill), and virtuosic novelties (such as a heating stove in the form of a suit of armour).
- Exhibits were arranged to permit each nation to show off its technological and artistic prowess, but there were two clear messages underlying the arrangement: firstly, that Britain led the world in technology and industry; and, secondly, that societies could fight their way out of the dark days of industrial unrest by inventing new technologies that improved productivity and beautified society.
- The average daily attendance was 42,381, with a peak of 109,915 on 7 October. This meant that over six million people – a third of the population of Britain – had visited by the time the exhibition closed. Given the recent unrest, the exhibition was an audacious move: royals around Europe, include Augustus I of Hanover, feared that the project would lead to mass violence and rebellion.
- In 1854, the exhibition reopened in a still larger building as a permanent venue in the London suburb of Sydenham. Profits from the original exhibition were used to found the Victoria & Albert Museum, the Science Museum, and the Natural History Museum. These buildings all sit close to the original exhibition site and next to the Royal Albert Hall in an area nicknamed Albertopolis.

The most dramatic symbol of this newly confident nation was the Great Exhibition of 1851. G.M.Young's wonderful long essay on the Victorians, *Portrait of an Age* (1936), summed this up. Radicalism and fear of radicalism, he wrote, defined the 'national mood' until 1848 when the great 'storm which swept away half the governments of Europe passed harmlessly over the islands'. 'The Great Exhibition', Young wrote, 'was the pageant of domestic peace. Not for sixty years had the throne appeared so solidly based on the national goodwill as in that summer of hope and pride and reconciliation. After all the alarms and agitations of thirty years the State had swung back to its natural centre'. Fear of 'the mob' disappeared overnight. Lord Shaftesbury wrote, in Manchester in 1851, that:

> Chartism is dead … the Ten Hours Act and cheap provisions have slain it outright. Often as I have seen these people, I never saw them so ardent, so affectionate, so enthusiastic … The Children look lively and young; a few years ago they looked weary and old.

Political developments, including the Ten Hours Acts of 1847 (which protected the rights of women and children by limiting the working day that could be asked of them), were significant in this shift: they made the idea that Parliament cared nothing for the working classes ring less true. Shaftesbury himself was a driving force in the Factory Reform Movement that finally made headway in the late 1840s.

However, the basis of this shift was economic. Economic policy in the 1840s had been based around a 'Malthusian' fear of population growth. The industrial revolution had initially led to hardship and misery rather than improvement. It was around mid-century that this situation changed. Between 1845 and 1855, Britain's imports and exports almost doubled. Real wages for workers finally began to show some small improvement.

The prosperous 'golden age' of the 1850s and 60s was based on transformations that had been silently gathering pace during the darkest days of class conflict. Chartism fizzled out in 1848 not because the aristocracy stamped it out, but because a general economic up-turn was slowly ameliorating the living conditions that galvanized protest.

ESCAPING 'MALTHUSIAN' CONSTRAINTS

The term 'Malthusian' refers to Thomas Malthus whose name is forever associated with a dire economic warning made in his *Essay on the Principle of Population* (1798). This held that sustained improvement in the standard of living was unlikely. Every time available resources increased there would be a corresponding growth in population. This increase in mouths to feed would soon negate improvements in wealth, and living conditions would deteriorate. This occurred because economic constraints (for instance, the amount of good land available to grow crops) guaranteed that expansion of resources would be slow and limited in scope, while population growth could happen faster. In the early 1840s, it had seemed that Malthus's predictions were coming true.

However, it gradually became clear that Malthus had failed to account for two factors that could overcome constraints on growth. One was coal power. This freed up land previously used for wood (fuel) or hay (feed for horses that powered transport). Investment in coal mining and in steam-powered machines soon promised a way out of the crisis. The other factor was empire. Malthus underestimated the scale on which resources from colonies, combined with new markets for British goods, would transcend the limits of Britain's landmass. By 1863, the registrar general could announce that there would never be any need to worry about starvation: food could always be imported in exchange for Britain's burgeoning manufactures.

As well as politics and economics, the rapid improvement of the 1850s had a cultural dimension: it is often interpreted as the triumph of middle-class ideals. The particular earnest, thrifty, and religious worldview associated with the early Victorian middle classes became a general aspiration. Employers and professionals were so successful at encouraging workers to pursue a bourgeois ideal of personal self-improvement, this argument runs, that Britain escaped the revolutions that ravaged Europe in 1848 and embarked on a period of unprecedented optimism.

Alongside championing the principle of 'self-help', middle-class philanthropists poured resources into organizations such as poor relief funds, temperance societies, hospitals, and educational bodies. These voluntary groups, a large number of which were founded in the 1860s, helped negotiate peaceful relations between the well-off and poorer labourers. Equally significantly, these societies began to give greater coherence to middle-class identity.

This was important because those who could be called 'middle class' had virtually nothing in common. They were divided by religion (Nonconformist and Anglican), by party (Tory and Whig; later Tory and Liberal), and by status (diverse degrees of social cachet were accorded to tradesmen, professionals, merchants, manufacturers, clerks, and attorneys). The voluntary activity of educational and philanthropic societies helped generate a sense of common purpose amidst this diversity. They were often organized by high-status professionals or wealthy merchants and run by more modest tradesmen and manufacturers. These multiple middle-class interests were united by one potent force: the belief that local and national prosperity rested on the stabilization of relationships between capital and labour.

The middle-class ideal of liberal self-education was given increasingly powerful statements through the 1860s and 70s. In texts such as *Culture and Anarchy* (1869) and *Literature and Dogma* (1873), the leading cultural critic (and chief inspector of schools) Matthew Arnold encouraged an independent literary and philosophical cast of mind among the educated classes. Arnold insisted that improvement could be achieved through the spread of high culture. 'Culture' was 'the best that has been thought and known in the world', and by making it universally available he hoped to 'do away with classes' and create a unified society. He insisted that the 'sweetness and light' of ancient Greek literature was the antidote to the angst and anger of the present. The middle classes were the crux of Arnold's project. If high ideals could be encouraged among the well-to-do, then they would soon spread to all; if they could not, then civilization itself was a lost cause.

A major step in Arnold's educative ideal was achieved through the Forster Act of 1870. Schooling had been a contentious issue for the early Victorians: different interest groups (particularly Nonconformists and Anglicans) had fought to prevent their rivals controlling the teaching ('indoctrination') of the young. It was a mark of the decreased tensions of the 1860s that these conflicts were finally smoothed over. The 1870 act established school boards to provide for all children aged five to thirteen. Boards would pay the school fees of the poor, meaning that schooling would no longer be the preserve of the middle classes. These universalizing principles were consolidated by a further act in 1880 that made elementary schooling compulsory.

If the working and middle classes gained cultural power and economic influence, political power was harder to achieve. In the 1850s, Marx and Engels both decided that they had been wrong to argue that the middle classes now dominated British society. Marx noted in 1854 that 'the feudalism of England' had not perished. A leading British radical, Richard Cobden, noted in 1858 that the aristocracy had lost none of their predominance: 'the middle classes have been content with the very crumbs from their table'. Parliament was, in many ways, still an aristocratic plaything.

At the same time, the growth and professionalization of a host of fields, including teaching, created a social structure that undermined the expectations of 1840s firebrands. These radicals had predicted that without drastic action society would split ever more neatly into the 'haves' and 'have nots'. In fact, as clerks, teachers, nurses, accountants, and a host of other occupations multiplied, the lines between gentility and labour broke down. In an increasingly complex society, growing numbers could not be fitted into the logic of upper, middle, and working classes.

This period was not all Arnoldian 'sweetness and light'. Multiple crises exercised the nation. The Crimean War (1853–6) caused much soul searching about Britain's place in the world, as did the Indian Uprising of 1857. However, these were experienced very differently by British people of all classes from the revolutionary agitations of armed protestors on British streets between 1839 and 1848. This was indeed 'a profound caesura' both in social conflict and in the usefulness of 'class' for making sense of society.

The rise of Labour

The mid-Victorian 'golden age' ended with the onset of a long and deep economic downturn after 1870. This recession restored class to the centre of debate. More than ever before, the conflicting interests of land, capital and labour were used to comprehend inequality and campaign for social change. This emphasis on class echoed much of the conflict of the 1840s.

The 1880s were the key decade in social polarization. As in the 1840s, the most extreme instances of the new class politics came in Ireland where Anglo-Irish landlords were challenged by the 'Land Leaguers' and Charles Stewart Parnell's Irish National League. Irish nationalist groups resisted aristocratic authority by inciting tenants to refuse to pay rents, sabotage hunts, and engage in direct action. This image of Ireland divided between Irish labour and English capital inspired powerful new campaigns for Home Rule.

On the British mainland, riots broke out in 1885–6 and large-scale industrial action in 1888–9. Strikes involved matchworkers in London, as well as mill hands, gas workers, and metal workers around Britain. As one observer, Thomas Lewis, put it, 'we are on the eve of a very serious crisis between Capital and Labour in pretty well every trade in the United Kingdom'. The most famous strikes took place among London dockers: an estimated 100,000 workers stepped out in protest against deteriorating working conditions and low wages. This moment saw the birth of a new form of Trade Unionism. Until the 1870s, unions had usually been small societies representing artisans in particular crafts. The new unions represented large, nationwide industries: membership rose from estimates as low as 140,000 in 1870 to two million by 1901.

This was also the moment when class became a party political issue. The Reform Act of 1884 increased the electorate far more than earlier reforms had: the voting population was expanded from one-third to two-thirds of adult males. Unsurprisingly, politicians were forced to adapt. Until the 1880s, Gladstone's Liberals had worked to safeguard the old aristocratic hierarchy, aiming to maintain social peace by introducing limited progressive measures, which were carefully calculated to prevent the development of working-class solidarities. In the run-up to the new Reform Act, Gladstone's rhetoric changed. He successfully reinvented himself as a champion of the working classes, affectionately known as 'the people's William'. A speech Gladstone gave in Liverpool in 1886 insisted that in matters of 'truth, justice and humanity' he would 'back the masses against the classes'. This was a statement of the Liberal Party's new stance. It is worth noting that Gladstone rarely spoke of the working classes, but preferred the more neutral language of 'the people'.

From this point onwards, the Liberals aimed to represent the people against privilege, while the Conservatives protected the traditional hierarchical structure against popular politics. Lord Salisbury, three-times Tory Prime Minister between 1885 and 1902, was happy to be 'an out and out inequalitarian' working in the interests of a 'divinely ordained' aristocratic system. For the first time, the divide between the leading parties in British politics appeared to be a coherent ideological split formed around questions related to class. This was therefore a key moment in the development of modern British politics.

The increasing ideological tension between different political factions can be seen in the rise of socialist organizations such as the Socialist Democratic Federation and the Socialist League. These bodies campaigned for working-class causes outside the world of Westminster politics, but under their influence an increasing number of Liberal MPs came to believe that the Liberal Party could never adequately represent working-class interests. In 1888, a Liberal MP, Robert Cunningham-Graham, left to found a Scottish Labour Party. In 1892, one of his allies, James Keir Hardie, was elected to Parliament as an independent representative of the labouring population. He soon founded the Independent Labour Party. In 1900, this organization cooperated with other socialist groups and the unions to form an organized Labour Party. Its purpose, in Ramsay MacDonald's words, was to 'arouse the labouring classes' to 'a knowledge of their power' and to wield that power to promote welfare and economic improvement for working people.

The Labour Party was quickly established as Britain's leading socialist organization, but it was highly unusual. Throughout Europe, robust Marxist organizations aimed to undermine existing political structures and replace them with systems more conducive to social equality. Britain was the only European nation that did not produce a mass Marxist party. The Labour Party was unusual because it worked within existing political formations: it competed with Conservative and Liberal politicians on their own terms rather than declaring those terms invalid. The influence of Marxist and Anarchist thought in the Labour Party's ranks was exceptionally low. Within the party, as in British society at large, most support for Marxism came from the middle classes.

In an article entitled 'Why was there no Marxism in Great Britain?', the social historian Ross McKibbin asked why the nation heralded by Marx and Engels as the seed-bed of socialism was the place where the spark of Marxist thought most entirely failed to catch light. Why was the creed that was intended to bring about the collapse of the capitalist system ignored by the labouring classes it was supposed to benefit?

The British social structure, McKibbin insisted, was ripe for socialist agitation. In 1901, 85% of the working population was employed by others, and 75% were manual workers: Britain was a working-class nation. Culturally, however, the collective attitudes present elsewhere were missing. McKibbin argues that distinctively urban culture and organization was very slow to develop among British workers: 'most sports, things to do with sports, religious affiliations, and many hobbies were simply ... souvenirs of country life'. Where many European cities were filled with blocks of flats, the British city was different, more like 'millions of cottages in thousands of villages'. Gareth Stedman Jones had already argued that this was not a work-centred culture but one preoccupied with sports, hobbies, and religious identities.

The image of Britain as a nation of factories was misleading. Industrial workforces were remarkably small. The average workshop in 1898–9 employed only 29 workers; even in the Edwardian period there were only 100 firms employing more than 3,000 people (even these often employed people on multiple small sites). The British were also slow to unionize: in 1901, less than 20% of the workforce was unionized. As in the working class at large, there was no shared politics within the unions: many members found the idea of socialism objectionable. All in all, McKibbin concludes, this was a culture 'without a unified communitarian interest and incapable of giving ideological direction to a working-class consciousness'.

Even when class reached its apogee as a means by which Victorians understood their social structure, there were still as many forces holding class identification back as pushing it forward. Class politics remained a niche pursuit and just one way among many in which people chose to interpret their place in the social order.

8

Performing gender: men, women, and the family

Think what it is to be a boy, to grow up to manhood in the belief that without any merit or exertion of his own … by the mere fact of being born a male he is by right the superior of all and every one of an entire half of the human race. How early the youth thinks himself superior to his mother, owing her forbearance perhaps but no real respect; and how sublime and sultan-like a sense of superiority he feels, above all, over the woman whom he honours by admitting her to a partnership of his life. Is it imagined that all this does not pervert the whole manner of existence of the man, both as an individual and as a social being?

John Stuart Mill, *The Subjection of Women* (1867)

Social class was one among many factors that shaped individuals' lives in Victorian Britain. Other considerations, from accidents of birth to religious identity, placed limits on a person's opportunities and defined their treatment by others. Among these many factors, gender was both the most powerful and the most complex.

Victorian society was structured by gender difference. Every aspect of life – whether access to education, opportunities for work, or representation in politics – was different for a woman than for a man. To be born female was to be confronted by a range of expectations, and a probable life trajectory, that was different from those that faced males in the same time and place. The Victorians conceptualized these divergent expectations in terms of a public/private divide. Public life, including the world of high politics, was gendered masculine. The private life of the home was gendered feminine. In this way, womanhood was associated with the nurturing of family and the sanctification of domestic space.

The Victorian domestic ideology that served to cramp women in custom, corset, and crinoline has been labelled 'separate spheres'. It has been treated as one of the defining features of Victorianism: a key marker of what makes the Victorians distinctive. The increased power of this ideology of gender difference has been associated with the rise of industrial capitalism. The emergence of large workshops and factories, it is argued, increasingly separated home and workplace. This separation gave new coherence to the world of familial privacy with which femininity was linked.

One question for this chapter is how far separate spheres was a genuine divide that dominated and controlled the lives of real men and women, and how far it was a flimsy ideal created by middle-class moralizers who were less influential than they claimed. The ideal of much gender history is to excavate beneath the well-known books and manuals that told men, women, and children how to behave, to reveal how they actually went about their daily lives.

There is no doubt (even among historians who question the power of separate spheres) that gendered inequality was just as real as inequalities of wealth. However, it is also clear that this inequality did not affect everyone in the same homogeneous, predictable way. This is why exploring the details and subtleties of gender in practice has proved so significant a task for historians.

CONDUCT LITERATURE

By the Victorian period, there was a long tradition of texts telling people – sometimes men, but more often women – how they should perform their duties and regulate their behaviour. These texts boomed in the early Victorian period: as the middle classes expanded, there were many who wished to appear respectable but had not had the advantage of early training by a governess.

They turned to virtual governesses: etiquette books and advice manuals. Therein, they read of the skills – such as sewing, singing, and playing the piano – that would aid the appearance of propriety and politeness. They found advice on deportment, posture, dress, and style that would encourage modesty and cleanliness. They read about norms for social behaviour, whether in letter writing or at social events such as balls and dinner parties. For instance, the (anonymous) *Handbook of Etiquette* (1860) noted that 'two ladies may with perfect propriety each take an arm of one gentleman, but one lady cannot, with equal regard to appearance, take the arms of two gentlemen'.

Some etiquette books and advice manuals were bestsellers, such as Sarah Stickney Ellis's series *Women of England* (1839), *Daughters of England* (1842), *Wives of England* (1843), and *Mothers of England* (1844). Ellis also penned advice manuals such as *The Dangers of Dining Out* (1842) and *Education of the Heart: Women's Best Work* (1869). Isabella Beeton's phenomenal bestseller *The Book of Household Management* (1861) shared many features with this genre. By the 1860s, texts such as Walter Gallichan's *Modern Woman and How to Manage Her* (1861) began to include limited advice on previously taboo subjects such as sexuality. As Gallichan's title suggests, these were often no less controlling of female behaviour and dismissive of female desire than earlier works had been.

Gender history is a relatively recent development and, over the last fifty years, it has done more to transform the ways in which historians approach the past than any other field. Until the mid-twentieth century, history was almost exclusively a matter of modern men writing about the men of the past. The extreme exclusions this implied did not just mean half of history was unwritten, but also that the approaches and concepts historians used were designed to explain historical change by narrating events in male-dominated high politics. Gender historians have rewritten history in ways that involve a thorough reconceptualization of what historians write about and how and why they write history at all.

This historiographical change is crucial to this book because many of the most important interventions in gender history have been made through studies of Victorian Britain, and everything now written about the relations between Victorian men and women is informed by fifty years of sophisticated historical revision.

A domestic ideology: John Ruskin's *Sesame and Lilies*

In exploring the gendered divisions of this period, it is perhaps best to start with a Victorian whose statements on the topic have been treated as typifying separate spheres ideology. John Ruskin was among the most powerful cultural commentators of the mid-Victorian period. He has long been treated as a pariah because of the stern vision of ideal femininity he presented in an essay entitled 'Of Queens' Gardens'. This essay made up half of *Sesame and Lilies* (1865). The other half of that book, 'Of Kings' Treasuries', presented a parallel vision of masculinity that has been only slightly less controversial. By the 1970s, *Sesame and Lilies* was used to epitomize Victorian anti-feminism; it was read as the polar opposite to the progressive *Subjection of Women* (1869) by the philosopher and political economist J.S. Mill.

KEY TEXTS IN THE EARLY CAMPAIGN FOR WOMEN'S RIGHTS

Victorian texts on women's rights had several powerful antecedents. The most significant of these was Mary Wollstonecraft's *Vindication of the Rights of Woman* (1792). This text was written in response to the French Revolution, which had defined the battle for democracy as a campaign for manhood suffrage and 'the rights of man'.

In the early nineteenth century, women played substantial roles in anti-slavery campaigns. Such campaigns were seen as compatible with feminine qualities, but they also led some writers to begin to equate women's roles in the home with a kind of domestic slavery. William Thompson and Anna Wheeler, for instance, published an *Appeal of One Half the Human Race, Women, Against the Pretensions of the Other Half, Men, to Retain them in Political and thence in Civil and Domestic Slavery* (1825).

By the Victorian period, the appearance of such texts was accelerating. In the 1840s and 50s, Flora Tristan penned protests against prostitution; Barbara Leigh-Smith attacked legal constraints on women; and Catherine Barmby penned a new 'Demand for the Emancipation of Woman' (1843). One such work – Harriet Taylor Mill's 'Enfranchisement of Women' (1851) – was by the future wife of the leading political economist of the age. In 1869, John Stuart Mill penned the most widely read of all Victorian feminist texts: *The Subjection of Women*. Mill insisted that 'the moral regeneration of mankind will only really commence, when the most fundamental of the social relations is placed under the rule of equal justice, and when human beings learn to cultivate their strongest sympathy with an equal in rights and in cultivation'.

The controversy surrounding Ruskin's text is increased by its phenomenal success in the 1860s. A runaway bestseller, it appeared in dozens of editions. It soon became a common gift for schoolgirls that could be found in many middle-class homes. One anecdote holds that when Ruskin lectured at Oxford (as Slade Professor of Fine Arts) women in the audience

> Recalled that their last school prize had been a book called *Sesame and Lilies* in which they had been told they must braid their minds as well as their hair each morning before their mirrors.

Yet many of Ruskin's reviewers in 1865 did not see the text this way. Some even saw it as 'an angry attack on traditional values'. Recently, historians and literary scholars have begun to take that perspective seriously and to recognize Ruskin's views as more complex than his reputation as a misogynist suggests.

Ruskin's essay presents the family unit as the bulwark protecting Victorian souls from the gross materialism of their commercial age. In explaining how the ideal family should be structured, he writes passages that are enormously condescending towards women. One of the most frequently quoted reads:

> Speaking broadly, a man ought to know any language or science he learns, thoroughly – while a woman ought to know the same language, or science, only so far as may enable her to sympathize in her husband's pleasures, and in those of his best friends.

However, far from providing the extreme assertion of separate spheres ideology suggested by this decontextualized snippet, other sections of *Sesame and Lilies* place great emphasis on female endeavour and seriousness. The literary scholar Deborah Nord insists that Ruskin was in fact protesting against a view of women as decorative and trivial, which he observed among the privileged classes. A particularly impassioned passage of *Sesame and Lilies* reads:

> Let a girl's education be as serious as a boy's. You bring up your girls as if they were meant for sideboard ornaments, and then complain of their frivolity. Give them the same advantages that you give their brothers – appeal to the same grand instincts of virtue in them; teach *them*, also, that courage and truth are the pillars of their being; do you think that they would not answer that appeal, brave and true as they are even now, when you know that there is hardly a girl's school in this Christian kingdom where the children's courage or sincerity would be thought of half so much importance as their way of coming in at a

> door; and when the whole system of society, as respects the mode of establishing them in life, is one rotten plague of cowardice and imposture.

It seems almost impossible to reconcile the first of these quotations with the second, and it has proved all too easy for those who use Ruskin to illustrate Victorian gender mores to quote only one. Nord argues that what *Sesame and Lilies* did was to credit the private conduct of family life with the power to combat the greed and competition of economic life. The domestic pair of man and woman, and the 'home' they combined to make were the site of resistance against materialism and exploitation.

This can help explain why the most enthusiastic reviewers of *Sesame and Lilies* were leaders of the women's movement who found in the text a rallying cry to a wider field for women's action. In an essay entitled 'The Feminist Origins of "Of Queens' Gardens"' (2004), Linda Peterson makes a strong case for a progressive Ruskin who drew influence from feminist authors such as Anna Jameson.

Sesame and Lilies demonstrates the importance of reading texts written by Victorians themselves: selective quotation can make a text like this into almost anything. It also demonstrates that readers should be alert to the conflicts and contradictions of this period not just when comparing the views of different authors, but in their approach to every text they dip into. All the oppressive power of separate spheres and all its fragility in the face of a complex society can be drawn from Ruskin's 'Kings' and 'Queens' read together.

The gender double standard and the Contagious Diseases Acts

While Ruskin was writing his equivocal text, a far more emphatic demonstration of the Victorian gender divide was passed into law. The double standards that placed different expectations and responsibilities on the shoulders of women and men were clearest in relation to sex; they were clearer still when prostitution was involved. The most notorious instance of this is the three Contagious Diseases Acts passed in 1864, 1866, and 1869.

These acts were an important moment in Victorian history. They illustrated new ambitions on behalf of a state that increasingly sought to intervene in the lives of the poor. They also inadvertently provoked the expansion of the women's movement, which developed rapidly into feminism.

The purpose of the acts was to reduce instances of sexually transmitted disease among soldiers. While servicemen's use of prostitutes was treated as a necessary consequence of the ban on their marriage, debilitating illness was seen as more problematic. After deciding that medical inspection of soldiers was degrading, the government instituted laws that permitted plainclothes policemen to identify women as prostitutes and arrest them. They would then be subjected to a fortnightly internal examination. Any women found to be suffering from gonorrhoea or syphilis could be imprisoned for up to nine months. This method relied on the subjective observations of policemen and took illness as proof of guilt; in so doing, it failed to distinguish between prostitution and any other sex outside marriage.

In one of her many seminal works, *Prostitution and Victorian Society*, the cultural historian Judith Walkowitz demonstrates how well-to-do Victorians conceptualized their society as split between clean, respectable classes and a world of poverty and squalor that was diseased and contaminated. 'Pollution', she states, 'became the governing metaphor for the perils of social intercourse between the "Two Nations"'. In this fear of sickness, the prostitute was made into the means of infection: she was the one part of the Victorian underworld that threatened to cross the sacred boundaries of the middle-class hearth. Confusing the distinction between criminality and poverty, the Contagious

Diseases Acts institutionalized social fear, the gender double standard, and social blame.

Domestic ideology played a significant role in the demonization of the prostitute. As studies of the sentencing habits of Victorian courts have demonstrated, women were either punished harshly or treated with leniency in so far as they conformed to the expected characteristics of ideal wife and mother. In the case of the prostitute, however, the gender double standard complicated things. Since men's sexual activity was rendered 'natural' and inevitable, the existence of a class of sexualized and disempowered women who were distant from middle-class life was seen as a necessary evil. By providing opportunities for male sexual release, it was argued, prostitution safeguarded the purity of domestic space. Prostitution was therefore seen as acceptable, while the prostitute herself was demonized.

Florence Nightingale was among the first to protest the Contagious Diseases Acts and their institutional sanction of male vice, yet it was only in the 1870s that concerted opposition arose. This activism united middle-class feminists with radical working men and women, and was soon labelled 'the revolt of the women'. From 1870 to 1886 (when the acts were repealed), extensive public campaigns sought to raise awareness of the double standard of sexual morality and the plight of those who became its victims.

Until 1870, the binary that contrasted the pious domestic angel with the corrupted temptress had received little interrogation. Women whose habits matched the angelic ideal were seen as good by nature, while women who behaved in any other way were seen as entirely and eternally corrupt: bad eggs from birth to death. After 1870, this essentialist vision was increasingly undermined. In literature, Dante Gabriel Rossetti's poem 'Jenny' (planned earlier but only published in 1870) recorded the confrontation between a man and a prostitute. This long poem turns upon the narrator's realization that, but for male desire, the prostitute would be as pure and uncorrupted as his own angelic sister. Rossetti and his peers in the Pre-Raphaelite movement also made prostitution, for the first time in centuries, a theme for fine art. In politics, respectable women such as Josephine Butler made common cause with victims of the Contagious Diseases Acts, speaking in Parliament on their behalf and treating them as sisters and allies in the fight against a hypocritical ideology that simply turned a blind eye to things that did not fit its ideals.

In order to indicate that the fault for prostitutes' conditions lay not with the women but with society, Butler rejected traditional Victorian terms for prostitutes such as 'fallen women' and spoke instead of 'outcasts'. Religious ideas had been fundamental to the construction of separate spheres, but activists such as Butler showed how religion and biblical language could also be a conduit for feminist thought. They argued that the degradation of some women was too high a price to pay for the idealization of others: it amounted to an un-Christian sacrifice of thousands of women on the altar of hypocritical bourgeois domesticity.

In the campaign against the Contagious Diseases Acts, many of the most prominent figures of early feminism were brought together around a common cause. The slogan 'Votes for Women, Chastity for Men' combined political and sexual agendas. Even those feminists who feared the entanglement between the battle for women's rights and questions of sexuality, such as Frances Power Cobbe, entered closer communication with a community of activists in the fallout from this galvanizing crisis.

It might be imagined that these campaigns were aided by having a powerful, respected woman on the throne. But Queen Victoria was not for turning. In 1870, confronted by feminist campaigns against the Contagious Diseases Acts, she wrote:

> The Queen is most anxious to enlist everyone who can speak or write to join in checking this mad, wicked folly of 'Woman's Rights', with all its attendant horrors, on

> which her poor feeble sex is bent, forgetting every sense of womanly feeling and propriety … It is a subject which makes the Queen so furious that she cannot contain herself. God created men and women different – then let them remain each in their own position.

The Contagious Diseases Acts provide one subplot in the complex epic of Victorian gender history. Women's involvement in economic life offers several enlightening counterpoints, many of which suggest greater freedom than the separate spheres model allows. For instance, historians of women's entrepreneurship, such as Nicola Phillips, Hannah Barker, and Jennifer Aston, have demonstrated that the female business owner was not an exceptional figure in commercial and manufacturing cities. Women who owned and ran businesses were not (as was once assumed) always widows fulfilling a custodial role until their sons came of age. Nor were they only active in 'feminized' trades such as haberdashery.

This is striking because, under the law of coverture (which persisted throughout the Victorian period), married women were not even permitted the right to own property. Their belongings, along with their bodies and souls, were legally subject to their husbands' ownership. In 'Women, Consumption and Coverture in England, c.1760–1860' (1996), Margot Finn catalogued several ways in which women negotiated wider rights than the law imposed. Since Finn's article, it has become even clearer that this law was widely undermined in practice.

Through analysis of extensive archival material such as probate records, trade directories, and insurance documents, historians have wielded the techniques of economic and social history to reveal social actualities that repeatedly contradicted middle-class ideology. The upper-working classes and lower-middle classes of Victorian cities were, it seems, much less structured by gender divisions than previous scholarship would suggest.

All these different themes combine to mean that in gender, perhaps more than in any other field, we see the Victorians contesting their own ideologies. This is the period of the women's movement, of New Woman fiction, and of the birth of feminism as an organized movement. These developments were necessary because of the sheer power of ideologies of class and religion that consolidated and institutionalized long-lived traditions in which women were subjected to the control and ownership of men. Any responsible use of the term 'Victorianism' ought to be compatible with the existence of Victorian feminism as well as with Victorian repression.

The historiography of Victorian gender

This chapter, more than any other, demands close engagement with the historiographical developments that have drawn its subject to the centre of historical debate. This is because Victorian gender history has been the key battleground in disputes that have transformed all historical disciplines over the last half-century. These debates are crucial in understanding what students and scholars of Victorian history do and why they do it.

The story of modern gender history begins in the 1960s. This was a decade of vigorous activism against elitist traditions of historical writing. The year 1968 saw student riots, which demanded new curricula across the social sciences. Campaigners insisted that history courses should include discussion of theory and historiography, and that history teachers should interrogate their own narrow worldviews. Marxist history was the cutting-edge agenda around which many of these activists rallied. E.P. Thompson, alongside other radical historians such as Dorothy Thompson and Raphael Samuel, gradually brought Marxist history from the fringes to the centre of university life. They founded journals such as *History Workshop* and *Past & Present* to challenge the conservatism of the established *English Historical Review*.

Women's history followed a similar trajectory to Marxist history, pursuing the same aim of undermining the primacy of high politics in historians' agendas. The first national conference of the women's liberation movement (1970) had initially been envisioned as a small history workshop; it was held at Ruskin College, Oxford where Raphael Samuel had established a vigorous new school of Marxist scholarship. Present at this event were many feminist historians whose works soon became the canon of a new genre. The editorial of the first edition of *History Workshop Journal* summed up this close relationship between Marxism and feminism:

> By bringing women into the foreground of historical enquiry our knowledge of production, of working class politics and culture, of class struggle … will be transformed. Men and women do inhabit different worlds, with boundaries which have been defined (and from time-to-time rearranged) for them by the capitalist mode of production as it has made use of and strengthened the sexual division of labour and patriarchal authority. It is relationships like that between the two worlds, between the sexual division of labour and class struggle, home and work, or the private sector and the public, the social relations between men and women, which form the substance of feminist history, and will enrich all socialist history.

In this movement, the feminist slogan 'the personal is political' was paralleled by the demonstration that the personal was historical.

Present at the first Women's Liberation Conference was a young historian, Catherine Hall, whose work would go on to shape how all three aspects of the conceptual holy trinity of social analysis – class, gender, and race – have been employed by historians of Victorian Britain. Hall began her career by analysing women's experience from the Middle Ages through to the formation of modern domestic ideology. This included an early essay on the history and politics of housework, which was both presented to History Workshop and published in the feminist magazine *Spare Rib*. In Hall's words, this study 'was concerned to recover a lost history and give value and meaning to the activities of women which had not been legitimated in traditional historical writing'. When she decided to study the nineteenth century, Hall turned to Exeter University. In 1975, this was the only place in Britain that taught women's history to postgraduates.

Hall soon began a decade-long collaboration with Leonore Davidoff, which resulted in the seminal text on nineteenth-century gender ideology *Family Fortunes: Men and Women of the English Middle Class, 1780–1850* (1987). In *Family Fortunes*, the comfortable Victorian family was presented as the site in which a ruling ideology was created. This ideology, on which middle-class respectability relied, involved conformity to certain rules of class and gender behaviour. In particular, it meant adopting the habits and language of the public–private divide. As Hall wrote,

> Definitions of masculinity and femininity played an important part in marking out the middle class, separating it off from other classes and creating strong links between disparate groups within that class – Nonconformists and Anglicans, radicals and conservatives, the richer bourgeoisie and the petite bourgeoisie. The separation between the sexes was marked out at every level within the society in manufacturing, the retail trades and the professions, in public life of all kinds, in the churches, in the press and in the home. The separation of spheres was one of the fundamental organizing characteristics of middle-class society.

Evangelical religion, the ideals of class, and the particular political circumstances of the early nineteenth century combined to validate a crippling ideology of pious, matronly, submissive, femininity. In Hall's words,

> To be a middle-class man was to be a somebody, a public person, while the essence of middle-class femininity was being constructed as private and domestic. Such oppositions acquired their meanings ideologically, but that ideology had material effects of the most immediate and concrete kind.

At around the same time as *Family Fortunes*, another historian of the nineteenth century, Joan Scott, published a short article that had an enormous impact on gender history. Entitled 'Gender as a Useful Category of Historical Analysis', this was a direct statement of many of the methodological concerns already being pursued by scholars such as Hall.

Highly esteemed by many feminist historians, Scott's work was criticized by other feminists because (like Hall's work of the same period) it moved the focus away from women themselves towards the relationship between femininity and masculinity. This has since been identified as a shift from 'women's history' to 'gender history'. Scott emphasized the constructed nature of both femininity and masculinity: there is nothing, she observed, real and inevitable about the social meaning of being a woman or a man. Every culture constructs these oppositional ideals for themselves, falsely imagining all women to have certain things in common, and all men to share other, oppositional traits. The task of every gender historian is therefore to analyse the ideological and institutional ways in which femininity and masculinity are imagined, consolidated, and enforced. This article became the second chapter of Scott's *Gender and the Politics of History*, a powerful exploration of the gendered ideology of both nineteenth-century societies and twentieth-century historians.

The new emphasis on gender as a social relationship necessitated the study of men and women in interaction, but also required the theorization of masculinity. Masculinity was a privileged category that afforded men social dominance, yet it also shaped men's behaviour in ways that could limit their wellbeing. One of the leading historians to have tackled this theme, John Tosh, has asked what the category of masculinity meant for men at home. How did the fact that the domestic sphere was gendered feminine shape men's activities in private? In *A Man's Place: Masculinity and the Middle-Class Home in Victorian England* (1999), Tosh takes seven case studies: an attorney, an exciseman, a doctor, a mill owner, a banker, a farmer, and a headmaster. He uses these to explore the rise and fall of Victorian masculinity, asking how individuals negotiated the often contradictory expectations placed upon them. He analyses the prescriptive ideology of domesticity, defining the place of the man in relation to ideals of devoted womanhood and a new emphasis on the special status of the child.

In a chapter entitled 'Father and Child', Tosh asks several questions about the nature of Victorian paternity. When Victorian ideology installed the wife and mother as the moral and spiritual guardian of the home, what impact did this have on the traditional protective role of fatherhood? Childhood was increasingly treated as a special, idealized part of life associated with innocence and vulnerability: as childhood was romanticized in this way, what happened to the traditional fatherly role of administering punishment?

In answering these questions, Tosh constructs four typical visions of the Victorian father's role. He labels these 'absent father', 'tyrannical father', 'distant father', and 'intimate father'. In practice, he insists, 'distant father' was the most common response exhibited by men whose role in the home was confused and under strain.

A related chapter in Tosh's volume analyses the socialization of boys in Victorian public schools, demonstrating how emotional responses that were now associated with femininity were discouraged amidst increasing emphasis on formal, militaristic discipline. As Tosh's vision of the 'distant father' implies, this emotional de-skilling had a substantial impact on the dynamics of family life. Elsewhere, Tosh extends his coverage to the manliness encouraged by late Victorian imperialism, in which military heroes, most famously General Kitchener, were mythologized into ideal types of hardened, machine-like masculinity.

This straightforward, inexpressive vision of masculinity reached its peak in the First World War, when artists and novelists lent their weight to the quest to achieve the total militarization of the British male. As James Eli Adams shows in *Dandies and Desert Saints: Styles of Victorian Masculinity* (1995), this was a very different discourse from that of the early Victorian period when the 'man of letters' had been just as prestigious an ideal as the 'man of action'.

From Catherine Hall to John Tosh, a great deal of work has accepted some aspects of the separate spheres framework while challenging others. This scholarship has suggested that, while many men and women did fulfil the ideological expectations associated with domestic ideology, they often had more agency to evade those expectations than pessimistic readings had allowed.

In an influential essay entitled 'From Golden Age to Separate Spheres?', Amanda Vickery made a particularly robust challenge to the power of separate spheres. She insisted that those who thought the Victorian period saw vastly increased oppression and division along gendered lines had overstated their case. There was, Vickery insisted, no golden age of greater equality to retreat from. Victorian literature and legislation formalized gendered divisions but did not create them. Moreover, the conduct literature that proliferated in the early nineteenth century was *prescriptive* rather than *descriptive*: it could be read not as a description of how things were, but as a wail of dismay from moralizers who saw women embrace the new opportunities of urban culture and aimed to prescribe new limits to women's freedoms. This left open the possibility that these moralizers might have failed.

From the 1980s onwards, an increasing number of historians undertook case studies in which the experience of particular women or families revealed exceptions to the apparent rule. Jeanne Peterson, for instance, studied the professional Paget family who occupied precisely the privileged middle-class status where separate spheres was supposed to be strongest. She observed that

> According to the received wisdom, Victorian ladies cared for nothing but homes and families, their education was 'decorative adornment' and they submitted to fathers and husbands. Three generations of Paget women do not conform to this. Their education was more than decorative, their relationship to money less distant than we thought, their physical lives more vigorous, expansive and sensual than either scholars today or some Victorians have led us to believe.

Slowly, exceptions like this began to amass until it became clear that not just a few but thousands of Victorian women owned businesses, published important ideas in male-dominated fields, undertook dramatic travel, and worked successfully in almost all conceivable fields. In Vickery's words:

> Where historians have researched the activities of particular individuals and groups, rather than the contemporary social theories which allegedly hobbled them, Victorian women emerge as no less spirited, capable, and, most importantly, diverse a crew as in any other century.

Some historians, including Peterson, have argued that these 'exceptions' are so numerous that the separate spheres model should be completely abandoned for some or all social groups.

Others, such as the leading feminist historian Martha Vicinus, suggest that, while Victorian 'women were not always the passive, submissive, and pure creatures of idealisations … neither were they completely free from this stereotype'.

What case studies have shown most clearly is that status and wealth could shape how closely men and women conformed to separate spheres. The very rich were able to flout convention; for the poor, one male bread-winner and a full-time female home-keeper might be a luxury that would end in destitution. The social stratum for whom this marker of respectability was both demanded and achievable was not, it seems, inordinately wide.

Most of the debates covered above took place between the 1960s and the 1990s, but gender history and two newer fields informed by its methods – the history of sexuality and the history of the emotions – continue to be sites in which powerful new perspectives on Victorian society are opened up each year.

Cultural approaches to history, which have become increasingly ambitious since the 1980s, have considered the personal lives and private perspectives of the Victorians to be a 'holy grail' of historical research. As a result, sexuality has become an increasingly significant preoccupation. What did these people, who were reputedly too prudish to say such words as 'leg' or 'ankle', really know about sex? How was that information circulated? To whom was sexual knowledge permitted or denied? How can we interpret the elaborate metaphors and evasions through which Victorians communicated about sex? How did those whose sexuality differed from the most traditional Victorian expectations conduct their negotiations between self and society? What psychological impact did all these issues have?

As historians such as Vic Gatrell have shown, the evangelical revival and 'civilizing mission' of the early nineteenth century closed down many kinds of communication about sexuality. Ribald jokes and dirty pictures were both more common features of the 1770s than the 1830s. However, as Michel Foucault demonstrated, the control of sexual behaviour and discussion did not involve total repression. In fact, it produced obsessive discussion among those who sought to regulate it: the Victorian period, Foucault insisted, was characterized by an explosion of debate concerning sexuality. From the 1860s onwards, sexuality was subject to scientific study in the hands of sexologists such as Havelock Ellis whose mission was to encourage rational and open discussion of sex. Historians such as Lucy Bland, Hera Cook, and Fern Riddell have analysed the work of these sexologists and the public circulation of their ideas to show where and when sexual knowledge was sought, how its circulation was encouraged or resisted, and what its social consequences were.

From *Doctor Teller's Pocket Companion, or Marriage Guide: Being a Popular Treatise on the Anatomy and Physiology of the Genital Organs, in Both Sexes, With Their Uses and Abuses* (1855) to Richard Burton's translation of the *Kama Sutra* (1883) and Havelock Ellis's *Sexual Inversion* (1897), a surprisingly wide range of texts could inform Victorians of the facts of sex. A key moment came in 1877 when two radical activists, Annie Besant and Charles Bradlaugh, republished an American guide to contraception, *Fruits of Philosophy, or the Private Companion of Young Married People*, written by the infamous atheist physician Charles Knowlton. They were put on trial for obscenity and inciting public immorality. The publicity surrounding the trial increased the book's readership from just 700 a year to 125,000.

Historians of the emotions have analysed the tensions between expression and control of feeling in Victorian society. This is a field that has been led by literary scholars, as poetry and fiction played powerful roles in training the emotions and encouraging acceptable forms of sentimentality. Nicola Bown has analysed the tears shed by those who read the death of Dickens's Little Nell, while Sally Ledger has conducted more general analysis of Dickens's emotional expression. Others, such as Thomas Dixon, have found intense emotional expression in unexpected places. Dixon has used anthropological approaches to decipher the meanings of emotional acts such as crying from judges in mid-Victorian courtrooms. The case study of a judge, Mr Justice Willes, who was admired 'for his prodigious intellect, for showing mercy in criminal cases, and for his tendency to be moved to tears' allows Dixon access to realms of the Victorian psyche and varieties of masculinity that more traditional approaches have neglected.

Much recent writing on historical methodology has demonstrated the great potential of histories of sexuality and the emotions and has established groundwork for their future practice. This all suggests that the roles of sexuality and the emotions in shaping the lives of Victorian men and women will be something we hear much more of in the coming years.

9

Back to the land? Nostalgia and modernity in late Victorian Britain

England is looking sober, prosperous, thrifty – as though the bad dream of the industrial revolution had somehow no more permanence … The dream is broken, the ugly nineteenth century has been wiped off the slate and the country has resumed its natural evolution from the eighteenth century, allowing for the changes necessitated by discoveries of science and improvements in the art of living.

Dugald Macfayden on Ebenezer Howard, *Garden Cities of Tomorrow* (1898)

Mid-Victorian prosperity could not last forever. As D. Morier Evans put it (see chapter 5): 'whenever we find ourselves under circumstances that enable the acquisition of rapid fortunes … we may almost be justified in auguring that the time for panic is at hand'. Sure enough, the last three decades of the century saw more than their fair share of 'panic'. An economic downturn after 1870 was accompanied by increased international rivalry to the British Empire, most notably from the United States and Germany. By the 1890s, industrial 'invasion scares' prompted fears that Britain was being overrun by German and American goods. Most frighteningly of all, it seemed that sectors such as the dyestuffs industry, in which the British had invented prolifically, were now being monopolized by German manufacturing.

THE DYESTUFFS INDUSTRY

In 1856, William Perkin, a student at the Royal College of Chemistry, had attempted to make an artificial version of the medicine quinine. He had failed, but had instead produced an impressive colour: aniline purple or mauve. The dye Perkin developed was applied to silk and other fabrics and became a huge commercial success. It was followed by other aniline colours, including a brilliant red known as fuschine. The rise of this industry was rapid: twenty-nine dyemakers exhibited at the London International Exhibition in 1862. Brilliantly coloured cottons, silks, cashmeres, and ostrich plumes were presented as a triumph of the application of science to industry.

Not just dyestuffs, but many German industries – iron, glass, gas, textile, and machineries – began by imitating British developments. Imitation, however, was often followed by a wave of superior innovation. Major German innovators such as Heinrich Caro and Carl Martius had served apprenticeships at British firms. Large German firms soon controlled more than half of world trade. Recognizing this situation, Perkin retired in 1874, aged thirty-five.

Several reasons have been given for the triumph of German dyestuffs. Some emphasize education: British universities gave greater prestige to academic science than to industrial science so that British innovation could not be sustained because of a lack of trained chemists. Others insist that the problem lay with investors: British banks favoured the safest investments, refusing to take a chance in unpredictable industries. A few explain German success through the actions of the state, which promoted industrialization, even providing state funding to aid ventures that were too risky or expensive for the banks. All three of these possibilities suggest that much greater integration between the interests of industry, education, and the state existed in Germany than elsewhere.

It was not just industrialists who were pessimistic about the state of the nation. Novelists bemoaned the soullessness of cities; they deplored that 'inner darkness in high places that comes with a commercial age'. In the 1880s, agriculture came close to collapse and the rural population declined sharply. Some commentators felt that British culture had lost its way: it was no longer the coherent, healthy thing it (supposedly) once was. This cultural pessimism was not just British: it was a Europe-wide phenomenon. The title of Max Nordau's bestselling catalogue of the ailments that afflicted the continent – *Degeneration* (1894) – says it all. When, in the Boer War, a high number of military volunteers were turned away as 'physically unfit', it seemed that cultural degeneration was taking biological form.

Over the last four decades, a host of historians have narrated this period as one of decline. Many have used attitudes to science and technology to explain the loss of British vigour. The British, they insist, are 'good at inventing but bad at developing': they rushed ahead in the early stages of industrialization just to fall behind later. British elites, these narratives suggest, are 'anti-industrial' and 'anti-scientific', therefore the skills of engineers have been undervalued. Among the aspirational classes, the lure of gentility proved more powerful than the profit motive. Late Victorian writers, historians observe, began to insist that the misery, squalor, and brutality of the Victorian city was not caused by lack of compassion or unjust distribution of wealth but by the urban industrial system itself. A number of those writers self-consciously abandoned the city, 'dropping out' of modern life and retiring to farms or communes in the Cotswolds, Wales, the Peak District, or the Lakes. This has been conceptualized as a movement 'back to the land'.

Because of this perceived shift in tone, many books about the Victorians come abruptly to a halt in 1870, 1880, or 1890; it is often different historians, searching for the origins of twentieth-century developments, who deal with the late Victorians. Historians observe that modern Britain is less central to the global world order than was Victorian Britain and sometimes choose to locate the beginnings of a transition from power to marginality in the economic downturn of the 1870s.

However, this image of decline is not all it seems to be. It risks misreading economic history, as well as mistaking a small counter-culture of anti-industrialist writers and artists for the mainstream of British society. As several recent historians have pointed out, the changes under way in this period are largely a matter of perspective. The economic historian Martin Daunton points out that, from a vantage point in the twentieth century, '1851 seemed a golden age of British superiority now under threat from the emergence of Germany and the United States as major industrial powers', but, if we were to think ourselves into the position of the early Victorians, then the second half of the nineteenth century would appear to be a vast improvement: 'a remarkable period of growth and prosperity'. There is also something unsatisfactory about reading a vibrant period of three decades as though it was simply a transition, less important than the decades before and after. The purpose of this chapter is therefore to ask whether the pessimistic image of the late Victorians as a people powerless in the face of their own onrushing irrelevance stands up to scrutiny. What other stories might be told of these decades?

The case for decline

The vision of British history as a story of decline was given its most powerful statements in the early 1980s. In 1983, every member of Margaret Thatcher's cabinet – the inner circle of British government – was given a copy of the most famous history book to have made this case. Thatcher and her political ally Keith Joseph encouraged their ministers to read Martin Wiener's *English Culture and the Decline of the Industrial Spirit* (1981) in order to comprehend how the economic pre-eminence of Victorian Britain had deteriorated into the mediocrity of the present. Thanks to Thatcher's high-profile advocacy, Wiener's book must rank among the most influential histories of Victorian Britain ever written.

Wiener argued that early Victorian England had been an industrial powerhouse. Aggressive modernizers from Richard Cobden to Samuel Smiles had nurtured and harvested the fruits of the industrial revolution. Victorian England was becoming the vibrant, thrusting workshop of the world and industrialists were beginning to take their rightful place as the new aristocracy. This was a golden age of growing productivity and fervid technological innovation.

However, Wiener insisted that this mid-Victorian vigour was short-lived. Achievements were never consolidated because the industrial revolution was followed by a conservative counter-revolution. Traditional forces including public schools, the Church, and a resurgent aristocracy conspired to foster a gentrified and anti-progressive environment. The skills of the engineer, the entrepreneur, and the inventor were treated as secondary to those of reading Latin, writing poetry, and cultivating artistic taste. Economic growth was sacrificed to an ethic of sentimental anti-materialism modelled on medieval chivalry.

The Victorian sages – Carlyle, Ruskin, Arnold, and William Morris – were the spiritual leaders of this act of national self-sabotage. Ruskin, for instance, recorded his desire to destroy 'most of the railways in England and all the railways in Wales'. The Arts and Crafts movement, championed by both Ruskin and Morris, fostered painstaking artisanal construction of furniture from expensive materials. The exponents of Arts and Crafts, like the champions of medievalized architecture, sought to resurrect the principles of medieval craft and trade guilds. They sneered at mass production and therefore at economic growth. This retreat into historic modes, Wiener argued, was a symptom of 'loss of confidence in the creative powers of one's contemporaries'. Rather than giving dignity to the working man, Ruskin and Morris's agendas put the brakes on the economy and undermined the nation's status as the global workshop.

Nor were these simply the ideals of grumbling artistic autocrats. Political leaders aimed to rouse national feeling by evoking the values of a bucolic British tradition. This was pursued most vigorously by the consensus politicians of the early twentieth century such as Stanley Baldwin and Ramsay MacDonald. Late Victorian novelists and poets, such as Thomas Hardy, also took a marked turn from Dickensian urban realism towards rural themes and settings. The stereotypical protagonist of the 1890s novel was a young man or woman who – in one way or another – failed to cope with the psychological impact of the modern, urban world.

The result, Wiener insists, was a mass illusion that industrialization was a bad dream from which the nation would awake. There would soon dawn a cleansed, post-industrial age in which Britain would be restored to its 'natural' cleanly and countrified condition. The British Isles would be, once again, the garden and sporting field rather than the workshop of the world. Paradoxically, the most urban nation in the world had begun to imagine itself as one large meadow.

To Wiener and his supporters, the late Victorians were obvious villains in a self-evident story of national decline. They founded heritage organizations such as the National Trust. They read and wrote unprecedented amounts about the countryside and the natural world. They instigated a 'folk song revival', invented rural mass tourism, and discovered morris dancing and maypoles. They founded magazines such as *Country Life*. Nostalgia defined them.

Wiener saw the economic impact of this culture of revival as profound and direct. When late Victorians flocked from cities to the countryside on day trips and holidays, rural areas became less and less places of production. Instead, they became the pleasure grounds that seduced the children of the great Victorian industrialists away from the industries championed by their more ambitious parents. One by one, businesses stuttered and shrank as their inheritors lost interest. Large numbers chose to live off acquired wealth rather than building businesses for posterity. The 'active' wealth of industrial capital was submerged into the 'passive' wealth of land and property.

Back to the land

The Wiener thesis rests on the idea that after 1870 'Englishness' came to be associated with rural life and that this redirected the aspirations of leading actors into unproductive pursuits. Late Victorian enthusiasm for the countryside *was* new both in scale and tone. From heritage pioneers, early environmentalists, and allotment enthusiasts to urban reformers, day-trippers, and intrepid expeditionists, a host of new forms of appreciation for the outdoors had emerged. It was in this period that cycling, recreational walking, and camping became popular. Many late Victorians saw the countryside as a place of venerable tradition, spiritual recuperation, and innocent pleasure. This was a far cry from traditional perceptions of rural areas as agricultural work-places or hostile wastelands.

Most of the major poets of the period were, in one way or another, nature worshippers, praising the outdoors with an almost pagan enthusiasm. Prose authors such as Richard Jefferies wrote rapturous texts extolling the idea of communing with nature. Jefferies ended his bestselling book *The Amateur Poacher* (1879) with the words 'let us get out of these indoor narrow modern days … into the sunlight and pure wind. A something the ancients called divine can be found and felt there still'.

Jan Marsh's *Back to the Land* (1982) provides a compendium of individuals, organizations, and movements whose efforts changed the meanings of meadows, moors, and mountains. Marsh chronicles the late Victorian emergence of places such as the Cotswolds as symbols of Englishness. She shows how a few prominent individuals made 'the land' into a profound political issue. They founded pressure groups such as the Commons

Protection Society in order to preserve public rights of access. They also aspired to take land from the ownership of wealthy private individuals and restore it to common ownership.

This egalitarian goal drew the attention of several leading socialists. The most prominent was Edward Carpenter, a Cambridge University tutor and curate who resigned his post in protest against 'empty intellectualism'. He moved to the hills of the Peak District in search of something 'authentic' and 'primitive'. He advocated total self-sufficiency, arguing that a dropout from city life needed only a few acres to end their reliance on modern society. His manifesto, *Civilisation, its Cause and Cure* (1889), attracted many prominent literary figures to his cause.

Another socialist, Robert Blatchford, made a similar argument concerning the need to protect and restore Britain's rural identity even if this meant the end of exports:

> First of all, I would restrict our mines, furnaces, chemical works and factories to the number actually needed for the supply of our own people. Then I would stop the smoke nuisance by developing water power and electricity. Then I would set men to work to grow wheat and fruit and to rear cattle and poultry for our own use.

The garden cities movement, which produced towns such as Welwyn and Letchworth, emerged from these sentiments, as did industrial model villages such as Bourneville in Birmingham.

BOURNEVILLE

In 1824, John Cadbury opened a shop on Bull Street in Birmingham, selling tea, coffee, and drinking chocolate. In 1861, his sons Richard and George inherited this business and, in 1879, moved their chocolate factory to larger premises on the outskirts of the city. They named this Bourneville. This site was gradually expanded until, by

1900, it contained 313 cottages in 330 acres. These cottages were homes for workers, as the Cadburys had taken it upon themselves to 'alleviate the evils of modern cramped living conditions' by creating a well-planned community around their 'factory in a garden'. George Cadbury explained his motives:

> The only practical thing was to bring the factory worker out on to the land, that he might pursue the most natural and healthful of recreations, that of gardening. It was impossible for working men to be healthy and have healthy children, when after being confined all day in factories they spent their evenings in an institute, club room or public house ... it was equally to the advantage of their moral life that they should be brought into contact with nature.

To this end, George planned that each cottage should possess:

> Eight apple and pear trees, assorted according to the nature of the soil, which, in addition to bearing fruit, form a desirable screen between houses which are back to back; twelve gooseberry bushes, one Victoria plum, six creepers for the houses including Gloire de Dijon and William Allen Richardson roses, wisteria, honeysuckle, clematis, ivy in a number of varieties, white and yellow jasmine etc., according to the aspect as well as one or two forest trees, so placed as to frame the building. Hedges of thorn divide the houses and form road boundaries.

Where labour in factories was seen as degrading, these late Victorians valorized labour on the land. Supposed traditions of English rural life – from maypoles to morris dancing – were reinvented and venerated as innocent alternatives to the bawdy, gin-addled music hall. As well as a fair wage, they claimed, workers were entitled to pure air, water, and earth. 'Indoors' became a dirty word. New organizations such as the Society for the Preservation of Ancient Buildings (1877), the National Trust (1894), and the Folk Song Society (1898) aimed to match the high-Victorian rallying cry of 'progress' with a new rhetoric of heritage.

The meanings and consequences of these developments are, however, less clear than they might at first seem. To begin with, the numbers involved in the impressive roll call of heritage organizations were actually very small. Many were societies of the 'three men and a dog' variety. Most Britons had never seen a morris dance or a maypole; most of those who had did not count them as a critical aspect of their personal and national identities. Of the citizens of Birmingham, less than 1% lived in Bourneville. The National Trust itself receives most of its significance from its later expansion. During its first decade, its membership numbered hundreds rather than thousands or tens of thousands. 'Dropouts' of the Edward Carpenter kind were necessarily counter-cultural figures whose actions were notable primarily for their extreme eccentricity. These figures loom large in the imagination of historians because they tended to be prolific writers. Carpenter, Thomas Hardy, and William Morris might have inspired thousands of their readers to make occasional visits to the countryside, but it is not clear that they had any appreciable impact on the social system itself.

In an article entitled 'Against Englishness', Peter Mandler argued that the supposed cult of bucolic English identity need not be accorded great significance. He made clear that 'swooning nostalgia for the rural past' took place 'only among a small, articulate but not necessarily influential' group of literary types. However, he also insisted that, even if British culture was suffused with nostalgia for a rural past, there would be no reason to assume that this had a direct, detrimental impact on the economy. Enjoying a novel about the countryside does not imply outright rejection of urban society: indeed, rapid modernization often goes hand in hand with the creation of myths about the national past. Thomas Hardy lived in a London terraced house while he wrote many of his most bucolic novels; his career relied on London's commercial publishing and industrious urban audience. His novels might have had rural settings, but they were products of a fiercely modern commodity culture. Equally, the new cult of the rural day trip relied entirely on modern technologies of steam train and bicycle. 'Nostalgia', it seems, was a very modern thing.

Peter Stansky's review of *English Culture and the Decline of the Industrial Spirit* suggested that Wiener had been taken in by an English act: the upper classes, in particular, maintained a traditional, nostalgic front 'beneath which ruthless profit hunting simmered'. Parliament was always packed with shareholders in major industries. Stanley Baldwin presented himself as a Worcestershire pig farmer whose factory would never sack anyone, but that was not how he ran his business or how he conducted politics. As Stansky puts it, 'the self-image that a person or country tries to project is immensely important in helping to understand the psychology of that person or country, but it is not necessarily an accurate or complete explanation of what actually happens'. The late Victorian quest to return to the land was not an anti-modern regression, but a product of advanced, industrial modernity that need not be associated with economic failure. In Geoffrey Crossick's phrase, 'only a truly urban Britain could really invent the countryside'.

Britain's economic performance

Wiener's narrative was developed to explain why the British economy failed so dramatically after 1870. His image of crippling cultural nostalgia was created for a specific explanatory purpose. Some of the most powerful criticisms of his case have come from economic historians who insist that the period 1870–1914 should not be read in terms of economic failure.

In the bluntest sense, Britain did fail to maintain the economic predominance that had fleetingly been enjoyed. Very gradually, Germany and the United States surpassed British productive capacity and grew into the largest economies on the globe. The

British share of world production and exports gradually declined: the world economy as a whole grew faster than the British economy itself.

However, if these relative measures are the sole indicators of failure, this poses a question: was success possible? Would a more economically focused society, with more profit-driven leaders, have meant that twentieth-century Britain out-performed twentieth-century America? Could the fiercely advanced economy of 1870 have continued to accelerate ahead of other rapidly expanding economies? The answer to all these questions is surely 'no'.

Despite Britain's head start, the human and mineral resources of the United States dwarfed British capacities: it was only a matter of time before relative positions were reversed. The question Wiener answered – 'Why did Victorian England fail?' – was misconceived. Relative decline was not down to British failings, but to the transformation of many other economies into equally efficient industrial systems.

Indeed, Wiener's question was asked as much to make a polemical point to its readers as for historical reasons. The British in 1981, he implied, were culpable in the undervaluing of science and technology: they needed to recover the spirit of a thrusting Victorian golden age before the anti-progressive counter-revolution had taken place. Here was a strongly positive use of the word 'Victorian', intended to conjure vigour, commitment, and inventiveness. The late Victorians, however, were presented as traitors to progressive 'high-Victorian' values.

In *Science, Technology and the British Industrial 'Decline'* (1996), David Edgerton endeavoured to escape pessimistic assumptions. He showed how manufacturing, technology, and industry all continued to expand through and beyond the Victorian period. After 1870, the number of scientists and engineers increased many times faster than the numbers in most professions, while expenditure on science and technology grew many times faster than the economy as a whole. In 1870, institutionalized science and technology had barely existed: the subsequent three decades were instrumental in their creation. Several profound technological transformations took place. In 1870, British industry still operated many sailing ships, but by 1914 these had been entirely replaced by steam. Large-scale electricity generation was innovated in the 1880s as was motorcar production. The late Victorians were, in fact, radical modernizers.

These inventions might have transformed the possibilities of travel and improved living standards, but the question of whether they caused drastic social change is less clear cut. Parliament remained in the hands of a wealthy landed aristocracy. As the French writer Hippolyte Taine noted when he visited Westminster in 1872, this was the wealthiest ruling class in the world, with power and landed resources sufficient to overwhelm industrial interests.

The repeal of the Corn Laws in 1846 had been welcomed by some as a victory for industrialists against profiteering landed and agricultural interests, but it had caused little immediate change. Repeal permitted unrestricted imports of corn, which it was assumed would lead to a dramatic fall in price. Unexpectedly, prices fell only marginally. There were several reasons for this. Europe-wide population growth raised demand across the continent. At the same time, the American Civil War damaged US production and reduced American exports. In Britain, new techniques of crop rotation and mixed farming did produce a more efficient and productive system, which, in turn, meant that the citizens of 1870 were eating better than ever before. The combined result of these changes was a profitable era of what has been called 'high farming'. Few could have predicted in 1846 that the 1850s and 60s would be a golden age for British farm owners, but for many decades after 1870 relative economic decline was masked by high – and improving – living standards.

However, from the mid-1870s, the impressive facade of the era of 'high farming' did, gradually, begin to crumble. The British market was transformed in the 1870s by a phenomenal growth in corn exports from America. In 1847, American wheat imports to Britain had been 1,837,000 hundredweights; by 1870, this had been multiplied by twenty to 36,191,000. In the same period, the price of wheat had fallen by two-thirds. The threat represented by the Corn Laws was finally realized and British agriculture, in the words of the agricultural expert (and peer of the realm) R.E. Prothero, 'plunged indeed into the abyss'.

The consequences of this were many. They included large-scale unrest among the agricultural workforce (the 'revolt of the field' as it was called at the time). Founded in 1872, the National Agricultural Labourers' Union already had 86,214 members by 1874. It aimed to challenge control of farming by the gentry and to end the situation in which workers were disempowered pawns on vast consolidated farms. In this system, it was argued, rent levels and land price had become artificially high because farming was used to support a hierarchy of British agrarian society topped by acquisitive aristocrats whose appetites were limitless. As in the 1840s, hostilities between workers, tenant farmers, and landowners were most intense in Ireland, where they soon began to be discussed as 'the land wars'. But throughout Britain new distinctions and tensions were opening up between different tiers of farming's elaborate pecking order. In Scotland and Wales, farmers and farm workers looked to the past, investigating ancient Celtic forms of land tenure as alternatives to the capitalized system of the present. In England, in particular, large numbers of workers considered farming doomed, and vacated rural areas altogether.

At the same time, the link between landed wealth and political power was severed. An increasing number of industrialists entered Parliament, and land ceased to be a prerequisite for sitting in the House of Lords: new Lords were not expected to 'give up trade' as had once been the case. Major landowners diversified their portfolios, investing away from their estates. Many, such as the Earl of Leicester (whose profits from his Holkham estate had halved) would have agreed with the character of Lady Bracknell in Oscar Wilde's *The Importance of Being Earnest* (1895): 'Land has ceased to be either a pleasure or a profit. It gives one position but prevents one from keeping it up'. Many, such as the debt-ridden Duke of Devonshire, sold off large swathes of their estates. As a result, the price of land fell dramatically at the end of the century and many industrialists were able to buy into the country-house classes.

Among the great beneficiaries of this change were banking families such as the Grenfells, Mills, and Barings who were increasingly integrated into the highest echelons of society. Finance now rivalled land as a mainstay of aristocratic power. Banks grew larger and more powerful, consolidating the City of London's position at the centre of both international finance and British life.

By the end of the Victorian period, the structure of the British economy had undoubtedly changed, as had Britain's place in the world economy. Several rival economies were growing faster than Britain's. However, only the United States had actually overtaken Britain. It would be several decades before Germany did too. Despite its travails through the depression of the 1870s and 80s, the British economy had not failed. For some, the loss of economic primacy might have seemed like an affront to Britain's 'imperial destiny'. But to those whose vision was less inflected by fantasies of entitlement, the economic rebalancing after 1870 was less unusual or remarkable than the strange circumstances that had previously allowed a handful of small Atlantic islands to extend phenomenal influence over much of the earth's surface.

10

Epilogue: history devastated in their wake

Victorian ideas can give us a clearer understanding of the origins of our present problems, showing how our tangles over education and class, gender and religion took root in the first place … they can serve a still more useful purpose in suggesting ways in which we can begin to extricate ourselves from our difficulties.

Dinah Birch, *Our Victorian Education* (2008)

Dinah Birch's insistence that we listen to the Victorians has been echoed in a range of different fields over recent years. Such invocations have praised the Victorians in effusive terms. Writers such as Birch are not suggesting that the Victorians 'got things right' but that they were unusually willing to think through difficult problems and to embark on challenging programmes of reform: we should be as willing as the Victorians to confront, rather than ignore, our most fundamental problems.

In this way and others, the Victorians are still with us in mind, body, and spirit. They act, perhaps more than any other period in British history, as reflections, refractions, rationales, and revocations of modern society. Indeed, the phrase 'we are the new Victorians' has become well worn as a celebration of industriousness and reforming vigour as well as, more frequently, an accusation of intolerance and backwardness.

The Victorians also remain crucial to the ways in which historians, politicians, and others narrate the development of modern Britain. The period between c.1760 and 1914 is constructed as the crucial point at which 'modernity' was born. Industry and finance replaced agriculture. Culture, society, politics, and economics moved from local to national formations. Modern cities took the shapes that we see around us. In the process (so the narrative goes), a new kind of celebrity politics was born, as were mass literacy and mass culture. The disciplines taught in schools and universities, and, indeed, the very purposes education fulfils, are also often identified as Victorian innovations. The division of political departments at Westminster, and the national, regional, and local structures of politics relate intimately to the formalization and bureaucratization of life in the Victorian era. In short, British people still live in a Victorian nation.

Not just the organization of Britain, but also the global order bears these Victorian scars. The legacy of nineteenth-century imperialism shapes many regions of the globe: struggles to escape the geopolitical impositions of the nineteenth century have been long and tortuous, and are often incomplete. Only gradually are the traditional names of rivers, waterfalls, mountains, and cities restored and the names imposed by Victorian travellers excised from maps. Victoria Falls is restored to Mosi-oa-Tunya (the Smoke that Thunders), and Myanmar's (formerly Burma) Mount Victoria is now recognized as Nat Ma Taung. Postcolonial scholarship, as well as peoples and politicians around the world, have worked hard to undo the divisive legacies of the colonial order.

The Victorians are present not just through remnants of their society that are yet to be swept away, but also through conscious revivals of their ideas and aesthetics. They are reimagined in the arts, literature, and social thought on a huge and seemingly ever-increasing scale. This phenomenon has no straightforward starting point: several examples can be found in the 1920s or the 1940s. However, the phenomenon has recently multiplied in scale.

The publication of one of the classics of the genre, A.S. Byatt's *Possession* (1990), marked the beginning of a surge in interest; the appearance of another classic, Matthew Kneale's *English Passengers* (2000), coincided with an even bigger revival.

These two masterpieces attest to a change in the nature of interest in the Victorians. Byatt's novel reconstructs Victorian attitudes and ideals, linking the late twentieth and the mid-nineteenth centuries through modern readings of Victorian poetry. It deals with the Victorians at home and in Europe. Psychologically astute, it conjures the Victorians as they thought and wrote more than as they acted. In contrast, Kneale deals with Victorians acting on a global stage. His Victorians include explorers who seek the Garden of Eden in Tasmania. However, with heavy irony, their quest undermines Tasmania's indigenous population and destroys the real island paradise they are exploring.

'Neo-Victorianism', as the trend to recreate Victorian society has been labelled, is now so prevalent that a whole journal (*Neo-Victorian Studies*) is devoted to studying it. A host of significant books have explored the ways in which Victorian society has haunted the twentieth and twenty-first centuries. Their titles range from *After the Victorians* to *The Victorians Since 1901*, *Victoriana*, *Neo-Victorianism*, and *Functions of Victorian Culture at the Present Time*.

Exhibitions have tackled similar themes, including *Victoriana: The Art of Revival* held at London's Guildhall Art Gallery in 2013 and *Spectres: When Fashion Turns Back* at the Victoria & Albert Museum. Even modern art has 'gone Victorian'; Grayson Perry's *The Charms of Lincolnshire Life* (2006) told the story of a Victorian farmer's wife's horrific response to the loss of her children. *The Secret Victorians: Contemporary Artists and a Nineteenth-Century Vision* (1998) aimed to uncover the Victorian sensibility behind a wide range of modern art.

Television, perhaps even more than art, has embraced the Victorians. This includes a phenomenal number of sumptuous

Dickens adaptations, which now have their own spin-off in the Dickens World theme park in the South East of England. But there have been even quirkier examples. In an article in *Neo-Victorian Studies*, Catriona Mills used half a century of *Doctor Who* episodes inspired by nineteenth-century Britain (thirty-one at the time she wrote) to show how visions of the Victorians have changed across that period. *Doctor Who*'s nineteenth century is typically a collage of literary images: the hansom cabs, fog, and gas lamps of Conan Doyle blended with the elaborate gothic strangeness of Bram Stoker and the theatrical characterization of Dickens (who appears as a character in the 2005 episode 'The Unquiet Dead'). Victorian spiritualists' claims to commune with a world beyond the terrestrial present are a recurring inspiration: several episodes feature tensions between those Victorians who are credulous concerning the uncanny, and those such as Dickens who look to Victorian reason and empirical observation to explain and neutralize 'illusions'. By later episodes such as 'Tooth and Claw' (2006), scriptwriters make great use of these two sides of Victorian culture: faith and scepticism, or, to put it another way, imaginative flexibility and rigid rationalism. They also appeal to the paradox of the Victorians as backward-looking modernizers: 'imagine it,' the Doctor demands, 'Victorian Age accelerated. Starships and missiles fuelled by coal and driven by steam. Leaving history devastated in its wake'.

One of the most striking neo-Victorian trends – steampunk – has imagined precisely that devastation of history. Victorian society, it might be argued, was constantly at risk of being destabilized by radical new technologies. Steampunk exaggerates that risk, asking what would have happened if technological innovation had been still faster while culture and style had changed very little. Where much sci-fi examines a possible future in order to understand the present, steampunk comments on the present by enmeshing incongruous elements of future and Victorian past. This takes its lead from Victorian sci-fi texts such as William

Morris's *News from Nowhere*, which imagined the distant future as a strangely refracted version of late medieval or Tudor history.

Steampunk recognizes that there are multitudinous ways in which a society can be 'modern' or 'traditional': these range from technologies of travel to moral attitudes, styles of clothing, political organization, or philosophical outlook. Steampunk treats these factors as a series of variables that can each be endlessly altered to produce unique combinations, each of which reveals vivid social possibilities. In 2009–10, the Museum of the History of Science in Oxford hosted an exhibition entitled *Steampunk*. The following year, the Kew Bridge Steam Museum hosted *The Greatest Steampunk Exhibition in the World*. In 2014, the Royal Observatory in Greenwich opened *Longitude Punk'd*, for which eight leading artists were commissioned to create new-fangled works inspired by the eighteenth- and nineteenth-century heyday of astronomical invention. With this kind of establishment attention, steampunk had arrived.

This is particularly striking since, as recently as 2007, steampunk had virtually no public presence. The first steampunk conventions were able to draw on fictional forebears stretching back to R.W. Clark's *Queen Victoria's Bomb* (1967), but the very first convention was held in 2008. The Victorians have been gone for over a century, so why has their aesthetic suddenly gained in popularity so dramatically?

It is a well-known axiom that science fiction is always about the time in which it is written. The crucial role steampunk gives to technologies based on steam, brass, and clockwork ought therefore to make us think about our own relationships to the technologies of modern life. Over recent decades, several transformations have taken place. Wires that once carried only electricity began to convey information. Technology then began to become invisible: information was carried without wires or any other tangible medium. The subsequent minimization of technology made it inaccessible, integrated, and unknowable.

It became impossible to replace the batteries in many electronic items; cars with complex circuitry cannot easily be tinkered with on a Sunday afternoon. Steampunk hankers after an age when the interface between humans and technology was apparently transparent. The Victorian period has come to symbolize a time when technology was accessible, when it wore its functions on its sleeve, and when any piece of tech could be modded or pimped by the amateur inventor, engineer, or electrician. In the light of this, technological innovators, such as Ada Lovelace (an innovator in early computing who has the added appeal of being Byron's daughter), have been added to the canon of great Victorians.

Yet technology is only part of the answer. In *Functions of Victorian Culture at the Present Time* (2002), Christine Krueger argued that a new era of global politics began with the 9/11 attacks. This moment brought back 'into popular consciousness the long – and largely Victorian – history of the "great game" of empire'. It 'did more than any cultural critic could have [done] to impress upon us the urgent need to address our role as heirs of continuous historical process'.

Krueger is undoubtedly right. The new tone of world politics has changed the way that nineteenth-century Britain is viewed. It has created new disagreements, and revived old ones, about who the Victorians were. Shortly after 9/11, a television series made by Niall Ferguson entitled *Empire* was aired, making the most strident case for decades that Victoria's empire was a net benefit to humanity. In Ferguson's view, this empire was an engine of modernity, pushing forwards globalization and Free Trade. It was, he suggests, an unusually moralistic imperial power that prevented the rise of empires that would have been worse.

As many responses to both *Empire* and the book associated with the series showed, Ferguson did not entirely ignore the brutality of empire, but his picture was oddly imbalanced: in the book, the destruction of native Americans by English colonists from the seventeenth century onwards receives two paragraphs, while David Livingstone is given over a dozen pages. In her review, Linda Colley emphasized just how divergent interpretations of the British Empire could be, and just how futile are any arguments over whether it was 'a good thing':

> Enquiring whether this or any other empire was a "good" or a "bad" thing is historically bogus, because answers to this question vary so much according to when, what, and who you choose to look at, and, critically, according to who you are. Focus, for example, on Britain's role in the slave trade in the 18th century, and its empire seems an early holocaust. But concentrate instead on how Royal Navy seamen sacrificed their time and lives hunting down other countries' slavers in the 19th century, and one can feel proud of Pax Britannica. Look at how the British covered India with railroads, and it is easy to view them as modernisers. Look, however, at the abysmal levels of mass illiteracy in the subcontinent they left behind in 1947, and they appear rather differently.

What has happened since 2001, and particularly since 2011, is that debate over the British Empire has become fiercer, more divisive, and more voluminous than ever before. The Cold War was not an issue with easy parallels in Victorian history. The major issues of current global politics, however, turn on questions that constantly seem to recall Victorian imperialism. These range from the activities of America, Britain, and other Western nations in Afghanistan and Iraq, to Russia's treatment of the Ukraine and China's foreign policy. Most of those who, in the last two decades, have argued most fervently about the Victorians have chosen particular views of Victorian imperialism that match their beliefs in terms of modern foreign policy. In an article entitled 'A Victorian Idealist in the White House', Ferguson set out his own vision of these parallels:

> Like Bush and Blair, the Victorians regarded overthrowing rogue regimes from Oudh to Abyssinia as an entirely legitimate part of the civilising progress; the Indian civil service prided itself on replacing 'bad' government with 'good'; while Victorian missionaries like David Livingstone had an unshakeable confidence that it was their role to bring the values of Christianity and commerce to the same 'people round the world' to whom Tony Blair wishes to bring 'democracy and freedom' … the left has made the mistake of assuming that the desire (in Bush's phrase) 'to make this world better' is mere window-dressing of imperialism, with the reality of economic self-interest lurking behind it. But this was and remains an oversimplification. The US does not stand to gain a great deal from controlling the oilfields of Iraq – certainly not more than it will cost to invade and occupy the country … the culture of imperialism would not be so enduring if it did not have some genuine moral content.

This was only the beginning. What followed the invasions of Iraq and Afghanistan were debacles of truly Victorian proportions. Like Gladstone's invasion of Egypt in 1882, what was intended as a swift surgical operation quickly turned into a messy, extended, and tragic occupation for which the people of Afghanistan and Iraq paid (and continue to pay) huge costs.

This created intense new public awareness of the moral issues involved in the intervention of one state in the affairs of another. Every single year, dozens of books on the British Empire in the nineteenth century pour from the presses. Some, like Ferguson's, claim that the modern United States should embrace its role as a world empire, while others show that there can be no such thing as 'clean' or 'benign' imperial power.

The rise of imperial history has seen a shift take place in our image of the Victorians. In the 1980s, they were an 'industrial people', as Britain and America worried about their post-industrial future. After 2001 the Victorians became primarily an 'imperial people': it is telling that prominent among the most recent works on Neo-Victorianism are Elizabeth Ho's *Neo-Victorianism and the Memory of Empire* (2012) and a 2015 special issue of *Neo-Victorian Studies* entitled 'Neo-Victorianism and Globalization'. This shift is a powerful illustration of the ways in which each generation creates the Victorians it needs, reimagining illustrious forebears as the forces of 'right' and 'wrong' in struggles that reflect our own. It is also, however, a reminder that we continue to live in a world shaped by those nineteenth-century forebears. In a century's time, people will surely respond to the impact that the people of the present have had upon the globe with the same mix of intrigue, attraction, horror and incredulity that we display towards the Victorians.

Further reading

Online resources (open access)

http://www.victorianweb.org/ – Wide-ranging introduction to themes in Victorian history.

http://www.digitalhumanities.org/companion/view?docId=blackwell/9781405148641/9781405148641.xml&chunk.id=ss1-4-5 – This is an excellent introduction to digital resources for nineteenth-century literature, written by John Walsh.

http://www.bbk.ac.uk/lib/subguides/artshum/victorian/Websites – A detailed list of online resources in Victorian Studies, from Birkbeck Library.

http://archive.org – Victorian literature, including thousands of novels, collections of correspondence (of, for instance, Charles Dickens), non-fiction, and poetry.

http://www.branchcollective.org/ – BRANCH collective provides resources relating to British history in the period 1775–1925.

http://www.19.bbk.ac.uk/ – Interdisciplinary studies in the long nineteenth century.

http://ravonjournal.org/ – Romanticism and Victorianism on the Net: articles on nineteenth-century literature.

https://networks.h-net.org/h-albion – Reviews and forum in British and Irish history.

http://www.amdigital.co.uk/m-collections/view-all/ – The company Adam Matthew has digitized several useful resources, on topics including empire, gender, and Victorian popular culture.

http://bl.uk – The British Library website contains several excellent resources, including the British Newspaper Archive,

British Printed Collections, 1801–1914, Victorian Illustrated Newspaper and Journals, and the Barry Ono Collection of Penny Dreadfuls.

http://www.oldbaileyonline.org/ – The Proceedings of the Old Bailey, 1674–1913.

http://www.prisonvoices.org/ – Prison Voices: Crime, Conviction and Confession, 1700–1900.

http://www.vam.ac.uk/ – Like the British Museum and several other collections, the Victoria & Albert can be explored in detail online.

http://webapp1.dlib.indiana.edu/vwwp/welcome.do – The Victorian Women Writers Project hosted by Indiana University.

http://www.darwinproject.ac.uk/ – Charles Darwin's correspondence (and more) digitized.

http://carlyleletters.dukejournals.org/ – Thomas Carlyle's letters online.

http://www.rossettiarchive.org/ – The complete writings and pictures of Dante Gabriel Rossetti.

http://blogs.ucl.ac.uk/eicah/ – The East India Company at Home, explores the British country house in an imperial and global context.

http://www.ruskinatwalkley.org/ – A digital reconstruction of Ruskin's St George's Museum.

http://www.neovictorianstudies.com – Journal dedicated to contemporary re-imaginings of the nineteenth century.

Key Victorian texts: a Victorian bookshelf

Victorian reading

What the Victorians read is just as much a part of their culture as what they wrote. Many 'Victorian bestsellers' were written decades, centuries, or even millennia before the Victorian period. The most obvious instance of this is the Bible, which, in the King James Version, adorned almost every Victorian bookshelf. At the beginning of the period, many people associated the act of reading with Christianity. Other devotional texts such as John Bunyan's *The Pilgrim's Progress* were therefore standard fare.

The Graeco-Roman classics held pride of place in many personal libraries (especially those belonging to the upper classes). Homer's epic poems *The Iliad* and *The Odyssey* were each subject to dozens of new translations across the eighteenth and nineteenth centuries. Prose writers from the Athenian philosopher Aristotle to the Roman historians Livy and Tacitus were also popular.

'The English classics' included Milton, particularly *Paradise Lost*, and Shakespeare. It is notable, however, that the works of Shakespeare popular among the Victorians were not the ones we esteem most highly. Guidance for 1880s school examiners, for instance, tells teachers only to test students on famous passages: one 'famous passage' they quote as an example is a now ignored speech from *Richard II*. Prose writers such as Francis Bacon and Thomas Browne, author of *Religio Medici* (1642), occupied a far higher status among the Victorians than they hold today. Charles Lamb's *Essays of Elia* (1823) and 'Dream Children' (1833) had quickly been accorded classic status. Later in the century, a wider range of myths and histories were treated as 'world classics'. These ranged from *The Arabian Nights* to Germanic folktales such as the *Nibelungenlied*.

The appetite for novels and romances had grown dramatically since the mid-eighteenth century, hand-in-hand with both the spread of literacy and the availability of cheap print. Jonathan Swift's *Gulliver's Travels* (1726), Daniel Defoe's *Robinson Crusoe* (1719), and all the vast output of Walter Scott – including *Waverley* (1814), *Old Mortality* (1816), and *Ivanhoe* (1819) – sold in vast numbers among the Victorians. Scott's poetry, such as *The Lay of the Last Minstrel* (1805), was popular, as was the verse of the Romantic poets. Byron was a celebrity with a committed 'fan-base' long after his 1824 death. Coleridge's *Lyrical Ballads* and the poetical output of Wordsworth were also important.

Many leisured Victorians were at home quoting several centuries of poetry, from Edmund Spenser's *Faerie Queene* (1590–6) to Alexander Pope and Robert Burns.

Selected Victorian writing

Cultural commentary

Matthew Arnold, *Culture and Anarchy* (1869), *Literature and Dogma* (1873)

John Ruskin, *Sesame and Lilies* (1864), *The Stones of Venice* (1851–3), *Modern Painters* (1843–60)

Thomas Carlyle, 'Signs of the Times' (1829), 'Characteristics' (1831), *Sartor Resartus* (1833)

Social commentary

Novels

Emily Bronte, *Wuthering Heights* (1847)

Charlotte Bronte, *Jane Eyre* (1847), *Shirley* (1849)

Anne Bronte, *The Tenant of Wildfell Hall* (1848)

William Thackeray, *Vanity Fair* (1848)

Elizabeth Gaskell, *Mary Barton* (1848), *North and South* (1855)

Charles Kingsley, *Alton Locke* (1849)

Charles Dickens, *Hard Times* (1854), *Great Expectations* (1861)

Anthony Trollope, *Barchester Towers* (1857), *The Way We Live Now* (1875)

Wilkie Collins, *The Woman in White* (1860)

Mary Elizabeth Braddon, *Lady Audley's Secret* (1862)

Lewis Carroll, *Alice in Wonderland* (1864)

George Eliot, *Middlemarch* (1872), *The Mill on the Floss* (1860)

Thomas Hardy, *The Return of the Native* (1878), *Jude the Obscure* (1895)

Robert Louis Stevenson, *The Strange Case of Dr Jekyll and Mr Hyde* (1883)

H. Rider Haggard, *King Solomon's Mines* (1885)
Mary Ward, *Robert Elsmere* (1888)
Oscar Wilde, *The Picture of Dorian Gray* (1890)
Rudyard Kipling, *The Jungle Book* (1894)
Bram Stoker, *Dracula* (1897)
Joseph Conrad, *Lord Jim* (1900)

Selected poets

Alfred Lord Tennyson; Arthur Hugh Clough; Elizabeth Barrett Browning; Robert Browning; William Morris; Algernon Charles Swinburne; Christina Rossetti.

Primary source collections

Kelly Boyd and Rohan McWilliam, *The Victorian Studies Reader* (Routledge, 2007) is by far the best general collection. Other volumes cover specific themes, such as James Moore, *Religion in Victorian Britain: Sources* (Manchester, 1988) and Tess Cosslett, *Science and Religion in the Nineteenth Century* (Cambridge, 1984).

Key general texts

Several books make useful next steps in exploring Victorian society, although most cover only part of this long period. They provide further material on almost all themes treated in this book.

G.M. Young, *Portrait of An Age* (Oxford, 1936) is a stylish, succinct book, which has been described as 'the greatest long essay ever written'. It offers a vivid sketch of Victorian politics and politicians.

The Oxford History of England covers the Victorian period in three large volumes. The first of these, A.J.B. Hilton, *A Mad, Bad and Dangerous People 1783–1846* (Oxford, 2009), is an exceptionally successful synthesis of cultural, social, and political history. The other two, K.T. Hoppen, *The Mid-Victorian*

Generation (Oxford, 2000) and Geoffrey Searle, *A New England, 1886–1918* (Oxford, 2004), are also excellent surveys.

Robin Gilmour, *The Victorian Period: The Intellectual and Cultural Context of English Literature, 1830–1890* (Harlow, 1994) is a wonderful cultural history.

Philip Davis, *The Victorians, 1830–1880* (Oxford, 2002) provides eloquent, impassioned advocacy of canonical Victorian literature.

Two volumes by Martin Daunton – *Progress and Poverty, 1700–1850* (1995) and *Wealth and Welfare, 1851–1951* (2007) – provide excellent coverage of social and economic history.

Jose Harris, *Private Lives, Public Spirit: a Social History of Britain 1870–1914* (London, Penguin, 1993) offers some of the best coverage of the late Victorians.

The general reading above is all relatively accessible and affordable. Part of the purpose of this Beginner's Guide is to make the knowledge published in thoroughly researched academic monographs available to a wider audience; this means that many of the works listed below are more expensive or scarce.

2. Sounds and sights of the city: experiencing the Victorian metropolis

Altick, R., *The Shows of London*. Cambridge: MA, Harvard, 1978.

Bailey, P., *Popular Culture and Performance in the Victorian City.* Cambridge, Cambridge University Press, 1998.

Briggs, A., *Victorian Cities.* London, Penguin, 1968.

Chinn, C., *Poverty amidst Prosperity: the Urban Poor, 1834–1914.* Lancaster, Carnegie Publishing, 1995.

Cohen, D., *Household Gods: The British and Their Possessions.* New Haven: CT, Yale University Press, 2006.

Crone, R., *Violent Victorians: Popular Entertainment in Nineteenth-Century London*. Manchester, Manchester University Press, 2012.

Gatrell, V.A.C., *The Hanging Tree: Execution and the English People 1770–1868.* Oxford, Oxford University Press, 1994.

Gunn, S., *The Public Culture of the Victorian Middle Class: Ritual and Authority in the English Industrial City 1840–1914*. Manchester, Manchester University Press, 2002.

Hewitt, M., *The Dawn of the Cheap Press in Victorian Britain*. London, Bloomsbury Academic, 2013.

Hunt, T., *Building Jerusalem: the Rise and Fall of the Victorian City*. London, Phoenix, 2004.

Koven, S., *Slumming: Sexual and Social Politics in Victorian London*. Princeton: NJ, Princeton University Press, 2004.

Nead, L., *Victorian Babylon: People, Streets and Images in Nineteenth-Century London*. New Haven: CT, Yale University Press, 2000.

Nord, D., *Walking the Victorian Streets: Women, Representation and the City*. Ithaca: NY, Cornell University Press, 1995.

Stedman Jones, G., *Outcast London: A Study in the Relationship Between Classes in Victorian Society*. Oxford, Oxford University Press, 1971.

Walkowitz, J., *City of Dreadful Delight: Narratives of Sexual Danger in Late-Victorian London*. Chicago: IL, University of Chicago Press, 1992.

White, J., *London in the Nineteenth Century*. London, Jonathan Cape, 2007.

3. Knowing Victorian Britain: the geography of four nations

Colley, L., *Britons: Forging the Nation, 1707–1837*. New Haven: CT, Yale University Press, 1992.

Colley, L., *Acts of Union and Disunion*. London, Profile, 2014.

Curley, T., *Samuel Johnson, the Ossian Fraud and the Celtic Revival*. Cambridge, Cambridge University Press, 2009.

Hobsbawm, E. and Ranger, T. (eds), *The Invention of Tradition*. Cambridge, Cambridge University Press, 1983.

Kidd, C., *Union and Unionisms: Political Thought in Scotland, 1500–2000*. Cambridge, Cambridge University Press, 2008.

Robbins, K., *The Nineteenth Century: Integration and Diversity.* Oxford, Oxford University Press, 1988.

Robinson, E. and Lawrence, J., *John Clare's Autobiographical Writings.* Oxford, Oxford University Press, 1983.

Snell, K.D.M., *Parish and Belonging.* Cambridge, Cambridge University Press, 2006.

Snell, K.D.M. (ed.), *The Regional Novel in Britain and Ireland.* Cambridge, Cambridge University Press, 1998.

Williams, R., *The Country and the City.* Oxford, Oxford University Press, 1975.

4. Knowing the world: the inventions of empire

Browne, J., *Charles Darwin: Voyaging.* London, Pimlico, 1996.

Edney, M., *Mapping an Empire: the Geographical Construction of British India, 1765–1843.* Chicago: IL, University of Chicago Press, 1999.

Hall, C., *Civilising Subjects: Metropole and Colony in the British Imagination 1830–1867.* Cambridge, Polity Press, 2003.

Hall, C. and Rose, S. (eds), *At Home with the Empire: Metropolitan Culture and the Imperial World.* Cambridge, Cambridge University Press, 2006.

Hewitt, M. (ed.), *The Victorian World.* Abingdon, Routledge, 2012.

Pang, A., *Empire and the Sun: Victorian Solar Eclipse Expeditions.* Stanford: CA, Stanford University Press, 2002.

Porter, B., *The Absent-Minded Imperialists: Empire, Society and Culture in Britain.* Oxford, Oxford University Press, 2004.

Qureshi, S., *Peoples on Parade: Exhibitions, Empire and Anthropology in Nineteenth-Century Britain.* Chicago: IL, University of Chicago Press, 2011.

Schaffer, S. *et al*, *The Brokered World: Go-Betweens and Global Intelligence, 1770–1820.* Cambridge, Science History Publications, 2012.

Stocking, G., *Victorian Anthropology.* New York: NY, The Free Press, 1991.

5. How cruel time can be: Victorian past, present, and future

Fritzsche, P., *Stranded in the Present: Modern Time and the Melancholy of History*. Cambridge: MA, Harvard University Press, 2010.

Gange, D., *Dialogues with the Dead: Egyptology in British Culture and Religion, 1822–1922*. Oxford, Oxford University Press, 2013.

Goldhill, S., *Victorian Culture and Classical Antiquity: Art, Opera, Fiction and the Proclamation of Modernity*. Princeton: NJ, Princeton University Press, 2011.

Lang, T., *The Victorians and the Stuart Heritage*. Cambridge, Cambridge University Press, 2006.

Melman, B., *The Culture of History: English Uses of the Past*. Oxford, Oxford University Press, 2006.

O'Connor, R., *The Earth on Show: Fossils and the Poetics of Popular Science*. Chicago: IL, University of Chicago Press, 2008.

Secord, J., *Victorian Sensation: The Extraordinary Publication, Reception, and Secret Authorship of Vestiges of the Natural History of Creation*. Chicago: IL, University of Chicago Press, 2003.

Secord, J., *Visions of Science: Books and Readers at the Dawn of the Victorian Age*. Oxford, Oxford University Press, 2014.

Turner, F., *The Greek Heritage in Victorian Britain*. New Haven: CT, Yale University Press, 1981.

Young, B., *The Victorian Eighteenth Century*. Oxford, Oxford University Press, 2007.

6. A community of believers? Religion in Victorian Britain

Brown, S., *Providence and Empire: Religion, Politics and Empire in Britain and Ireland, 1815–1914*. Basingstoke, Routledge, 2008.

Hilton, A.J.B., *The Age of Atonement: The Influence of Evangelicalism on Social and Economic Thought 1785–1865*. Oxford, Oxford University Press, 1986.

Katz, D., *God's Last Words: the English Bible from the Reformation to Fundamentalism*. New Haven: CT,Yale University Press, 2004.
Larsen, T., *Crisis of Doubt: Honest Faith in Nineteenth-Century England*. Oxford, Oxford University Press, 2008.
Larsen,T., *A People of One Book: the Bible and the Victorians*. Oxford, Oxford University Press, 2012.
McLeod, H., *Religion and Society in England, 1850–1914*. Basingstoke, Palgrave Macmillan, 1996.
Owen, A., *The Place of Enchantment: British Occultism and the Culture of the Modern*. Chicago: IL, University of Chicago Press, 2004.
Snell, K.D.M and Ell, P., *Rival Jerusalems: the Geography of Victorian Religion*. Cambridge, Cambridge University Press, 2000.
Turner, F., *Contesting Cultural Authority: Essays in Victorian Intellectual Life*. Cambridge, Cambridge University Press, 1993.
Wheeler, M., *Old Enemies: Catholic and Protestant in Nineteenth-Century Culture*. Oxford, Oxford University Press, 2006.
Wolffe, J., *God and Greater Britain: Religion and National Life in Britain and Ireland, 1843–1945*. Basingstoke, Routledge, 1994.

7. Reforming class: politics and the social order

Cannadine, D., *Class in Britain*. London, Penguin, 1998.
Joyce, P., *Visions of the People: Industrial England and the Question of Class c.1848–1914*. Cambridge, Cambridge University Press, 1993.
Joyce, P., *Democratic Subjects: The Self and the Social in Nineteenth-Century England*. Cambridge, Cambridge University Press, 1994.
Joyce, P., *Class*. Oxford, Oxford University Press, 1995.
McKibbin, R., *The Ideologies of Class: Social Relations in Britain 1880–1950*. Oxford, Oxford University Press, 1994.
Miles, A. and Savage, M., *The Remaking of the British Working Class, 1840–1940*. Abingdon, Routledge, 1994.

Moretti, F., *The Bourgeois: Between History and Literature*. London, Verso Books, 2013.

Morris, R.J., *Men, Women and Property in England 1780–1870*. Cambridge, Cambridge University Press, 2005.

Pickering, P., *Chartism and the Chartists in Manchester and Salford*. Basingstoke, Palgrave Macmillan, 1995.

Poovey, M., *Making a Social Body: British Cultural Formation 1830–1914*. Chicago: IL, University of Chicago Press, 1995.

Reid, A., *United We Stand: A History of Britain's Trade Unions*. London, Penguin, 2004.

Stedman Jones, G., *Languages of Class: Studies in English Working-Class History 1832–1982*. Cambridge, Cambridge University Press, 1983.

Thompson, E.P., *The Making of the English Working Class*. London, Penguin, 1963.

Wahrman, D., *Imagining the Middle Class: The Political Representation of Class in Britain, c.1780–1840*. Cambridge, Cambridge University Press, 1995.

8. Performing gender: men, women, and the family

Adams, J.E., *Dandies and Desert Saints: Styles of Victorian Masculinity*. Ithaca: NY, Cornell University Press, 1995.

Barker, H., *The Business of Women: Female Enterprise and Urban Development in Northern England 1760–1830*. Oxford, Oxford University Press, 2006.

Cocks, H. and Houlbrook, M., *Palgrave Advances in the Modern History of Sexuality*. Basingstoke, Palgrave, 2005.

Davidoff, L. and Hall, C., *Family Fortunes: Men and Women of the English Middle Class 1780–1850*. Abingdon, Routledge, 1987.

Hall, C., *White, Male and Middle Class: Explorations in Feminism and History*. Oxford, Polity, 1992.

Levine, P., *Victorian Feminism, 1850–1900*. Gainesville: FL, University Press of Florida, 1990.

Mason, M., *The Making of Victorian Sexual Attitudes.* Oxford, Oxford University Press, 1994.

Marcus, S., *Between Women: Friendship, Desire and Marriage in Victorian England.* Princeton: NJ, Princeton University Press, 2006.

Morgan, S., *A Victorian Woman's Place: Public Culture in the Nineteenth Century.* London, I.B. Tauris, 2007.

Phillips, N., *Women in Business, 1700–1850.* Woodbridge, Boydell, 2006.

Rose, S., *What is Gender History?* Oxford, Polity, 2010.

Scott, J.W., *Gender and the Politics of History.* New York: NY, Columbia University Press, 1989.

Tosh, J., *A Man's Place: Masculinity and the Middle-Class Home in Victorian England.* New Haven: CT, Yale University Press, 1999.

Vicinus, M., *Suffer and Be Still: Women in the Victorian Age.* London, Methuen, 1980.

Walkowitz, J., *City of Dreadful Delight: Narratives of Sexual Danger in Late-Victorian London.* Chicago: IL, University of Chicago Press, 2013.

9. Back to the land? Nostalgia and modernity in late Victorian Britain

Bonnett, A., *Left in the Past: Radicalism and the Politics of Nostalgia.* New York, Continuum, 2010.

Edgerton, D., *Science, Technology and the British Industrial 'Decline', 1870–1970.* Cambridge, Cambridge University Press, 1996.

Mandler, P., *The Fall and Rise of the Stately Home.* New Haven: CT, Yale University Press, 1997.

Marsh, J., *Back to the Land.* London, Quartet Books, 1982.

Rubinstein, W.D., *Capitalism, Culture and Decline in Britain.* Basingstoke, Routledge, 1994.

Walton, J.K., *The English Seaside Resort: a Social History, 1750–1914.* Leicester, Leicester University Press, 1983.

Wiener, M., *English Culture and the Decline of the Industrial Spirit.* Cambridge, Cambridge University Press, 1981.

10. Epilogue: history devastated in their wake

Birch, B., *Our Victorian Education.* Oxford, Blackwell, 2008.

Feldman, M. and Schaffner, I., *The Secret Victorians: Contemporary Artists and a Nineteenth-Century Vision.* London, National Touring Exhibitions, 1998.

Heilmann, A. and Llewellyn, M., *Neo-Victorianism: the Victorians in the Twenty-First Century, 1999–2009.* Basingstoke, Palgrave Macmillan, 2010.

Ho, E., *Neo-Victorianism and the Memory of Empire.* London, Bloomsbury, 2012.

Kaplan, C., *Victoriana: Histories, Fictions, Criticisms.* Edinburgh, Edinburgh University Press, 2007.

Krueger, C., *Functions of Victorian Culture at the Present Time.* Athens: OH, Ohio University Press, 2002.

Mandler, P. and Pedersen, S., *After the Victorians: Private Conscience and Public Duty in Modern Britain.* Basingstoke, Routledge, 2005.

Primorac, A. and Pietrzak-Franger, M. (eds), *Neo-Victorian Studies*, Special Issue, 8:1 (2015): Neo-Victorianism and Globalization.

Taylor, M. and Wolff, M., *The Victorians Since 1901: Histories, Representations and Revisions.* Manchester, Manchester University Press, 2004.

Index